THE CLEAR-MINDED

LEADER

3 Powerful Steps to Develop the Mindset of Authentic and Successful Leaders

CARLOS GOMEZ

CONTENT

"Want to be an authentic and successful leader?
Value human beings above all else!"

-Carlos Gomez

FOREWORD

The Clear-minded Leader is a must-have to everyone who is yet to find the key to long-lasting success in life. If you are like most of us in searching for that one tool kit to help you make long-lasting changes, go no further. The Clear-minded Leader is the one book you need. It uniquely combines spiritual elements with practical advices and provides proven steps to help us all.

Having read myriad books on success and mindfulness, I have found that there are two kinds of books in the market. Books that take you to a spiritual journey to success; and books that are all about making millions in a week, month, year or though changing your lifestyle and modelling others who already accomplished it. Although I have found great advices in both types, I struggled to fully embed the changes in my life; they were either too abstract for my everyday work-family-home reality or too mechanical and impersonal for me to able to adapt in my life.

In the midst of my search for finding success, I met Carlos. He saw my disillusionment with myself and started coaching me by giving me the simplest but most effective advices. Carlos is a natural-born coach and he has the strongest passion to helping others. His passion is apparent in his ever-growing curiosity and drive to understand my motives, beliefs and setbacks that I set for myself. It was through his coaching sessions that I understood what is holding me back in life and why and it was through is coaching that I overcame these barriers. Make no mistake, this is not an easy journey but it is certainly a life changing one.

Carlos began his extensive research into understanding how we can make changes last and, most importantly, how we can make those individual changes that are unique to us. He has built up a knowledge that is unique in this field as it is as spiritual as it is practical and easy to follow. The great advantage of his method is that he starts with help us understand why we do things in a certain way and how we can change it. He then helps formulate knowledge that we already have and turn it into a training tool, which ultimately takes us to a state, where achieving our goals happen organically. The Clear-minded Leader is not only a tool kit but it is a comprehensive programme that explains in what order we must take our steps toward success and why that order cannot be changed.

It is my utmost pleasure to recommend this book, as I know, it will benefit thousands if not millions of people around the globe. I am the living example that his method works and that his practical, logical and easy-to-follow framework is applicable to all walks of life. I close my forward with the single most powerful message from Carlos that he repeated to me until I believed myself, "I believe you can; I believe you will be the best version of yourself, I believe in you!"

With deepest gratitude and honour to all the help and support that I received from Carlos;

Thank you,
Viktoria Gal

WHY I WROTE THIS BOOK AND WHY YOU SHOULD READ IT

"No one can help someone else at less that person is willing to be helped, but still he must change by himself only with his own effort."

-James Allen

1985

It was nearly Christmas time. I was 11 and it was my very first day as the head of my family. My mum was diagnosed with a chronic kidney disease and the treatment was not available in our hometown; my two little sisters, my mum and I had to quickly move to a different city as her life was suddenly at high risk, while my dad had to stay behind for his job. In a matter of hours, my family literarily broke apart and we were facing the most uncertain time of our lives.

Somehow, as I was the eldest, I was given, or at least I "felt", the responsibility to look after my family and myself during the weekdays and wait for my dad to visit us every weekend.

The very first Sunday afternoon my dad left was one of the saddest days in my life; we all felt completely lost. I saw emptiness in my mum's eyes. At that moment she asked me to come closer to her and told me that the doctor thought it would take six months for her to have a kidney transplant and then we would be back to our normal life. Very little did we know at that time that this situation would last for almost twelve years. However, right then I thought it would only be six months to see my family reunited and happy again. That was my VISION, which was my DRIVE.

That same afternoon, she opened a small bag and took out my old

3

boy scouts' cap. We both looked at it and many happy moments came to my mind; however, what my mum was giving me "with or without intention" (I really don't know) was a physical symbol of a set of values, including a very strong sense of PURPOSE. She asked me if I remembered what a good boy scout did?... and in no time I shouted "I SERVE OTHERS!"... and what are your values, she asked? But when she saw in my eyes that I was ready to confidently reply with each and every single scouts' value I had taken as my own personal qualities she stopped me, she hugged me and she smiled at me. Again, I do not know if it was her intention but with that action, she simply set for me the most powerful source of psychological and spiritual ENERGY.

For five years and until the day I graduated from high school, I did my best to fulfil my duty to my family and to God. It never occurred to me to question my life situation, I simply obeyed and ignored whether there was any underlying reason. I was CONVINCED I had a mission to help my family. I never questioned it; for me it was a natural belief that I had to help others every time anyone needed help. I guess my mum and dad implanted those values and beliefs very early in my life.

For me, every little task was a mission to be accomplished. Sometimes, and despite my young age, I had to take buses and go far away to places in a city I barely knew. I remember going to banks or state agencies and having to talk to adults and many times I was the only one receiving my mum's hospital treatment report regarding her deteriorating condition. By the age of fourteen, I had a special driving license for underage people - very helpful when rushing my mum to the hospital late at night as she constantly had asthma attacks. This was all very heavy stuff for a boy of my age. It was like that for the following eleven years. By far the most painful activity I had to do during my teens was to carry my mum upstairs to the fourth floor to our flat when she felt too weak to walk by herself (at that time her weight was just below 40Kg due to her illness). I served my family for almost five years with no other INTENTION but our well-being.

What kept me going? Apart of the love for my family, of course. Simply, the extraordinary energy that emerged from having a focused vision, the purpose that was driving me, the set of values and a strong character that my parents helped me to build during my childhood.

I now realise I had the right mindset at that time, the right belief system. I valued myself. I considered myself worthy and of course I accepted it and was comfortable with who I was. I was building a strong character, therefore, I felt confident and truly believed in myself. Me and even my two little sisters felt empowered, physically stronger and morally straight. My mum felt it too, thus she wanted me to go to a good university in another city to develop my full potential. I was filled with a strong self-belief I was up to the challenge. My sister took care of my mum from that moment and with exactly the same mindset. She even did a better job.

A few years later, life changed; my mum died.

The level of UNCERTAINTY was higher. This difficult situation in life of losing my mum was so devastating that it affected me in many other aspects of my being, particularly in my professional career. When she died, a big part of myself also went. I was left with no vision, no purpose and most of my fundamental beliefs vanished slowly but progressively. After a couple of years, I completely forgot who I used to be. I started losing confidence in myself; my self-esteem and self-belief also dropped and with it my positive mental attitude, which was then replaced with an ever increasing negative attitude, fear and anxiety. The worst of it is the fact that I never realised what was happening. So it could only get worse and worse.

Since 1997, and for more than ten years, I tried to deal with this situation but I failed. I worked for different companies in different roles under different managers but with a new vision: to build a "high-flying" career. From junior roles to senior management positions, I managed to achieve some positive results and with pain and hard work I began to build my career, stepping up to higher positions.

Even though I had all the academic qualifications, skills and experience, I felt something wasn't right or at least something was missing. I was showing others a strong face and built an image of

5

success according to my role and other people's expectations. However, inside my mind I was suffering. I never felt totally comfortable in any role, company or position.

Every time I had a new higher position, the feeling of success was quickly overtaken by fear, worry and anxiety. Just like for many other people, these negative feeling grew on a daily basis and destroyed my self-confidence. I continued having doubts about my skills and my own capabilities and became so nervous that doing simple tasks or making some decisions were becoming harder every day.

Due to the sort of thoughts I was entertaining in my mind as well as my constant negative emotional state, I felt I was becoming a fearful leader with a weakened character. This lack of self-belief, clarity and confidence meant I couldn't perform at my top level in any of these roles and responsibilities. I never felt totally in control, neither of the situation nor of myself. I was losing motivation and my aim of being a high flyer and high performer was diluting.

As professional and later as a manager, I had a constant fear of not being highly effective, a fear of making mistakes and letting my team down and ultimately losing my job. When giving orders, I feared what others might think of me or my decisions. I feared being discriminated against and humiliated for whatever reason. I became used to checking others' behaviours and attitudes towards me and made my own interpretation, as if I wasn't worthy of their acceptance or approval. I had constant feelings of inferiority and allowed others to put me down. I was taking unfair or misguided criticism to heart; I could not control criticism. I could no longer connect deeply with others. Later I understood I sadly became dependent on others' acknowledgement to give me the feeling that I was of value. I stopped serving others and was driven by self-interest.

When are they going to sack me? How long will I resist this situation? What I am going to do with no job? Am I ever going to find a good job again? I am not competent...and those sorts of thoughts were continuously present in my mind. My mind was constantly somewhere else, just wondering around with these negative thoughts and feelings. I was totally unable to control negative thoughts and negative self-talk.

Many days, particularly Mondays, I used to feel more and more dragged down as I was getting closer to the office. I remember walking to my cubicle, sighing the Monday morning sigh to my colleagues and dropping my documents with a thud that, to me, sounded like prison cell doors closing behind me. Put simply, I was not doing what I really wanted to do. I felt physically and mentally tired. I had no more energy.

My attitude to work changed completely. I began hating Monday and I was simply going through the week looking forward to the weekends. As a result, some of my good habits such as punctuality and walking the extra mile changed. Part of me wanted to do a great job and fight for my dreams, but the other side hated the job and the way I was doing it. My fears became worries that, bit by bit and without me noticing, were affecting my attention and concentration levels and my productivity and professional performance in general were decreasing. Just like an endless circle, these situations were again feeding my mind with more negative thoughts. At that time, my mind was so passive and disturbed that I ended up becoming very anxious at work. My standards were lower and reaching high performance at work was not easy under that mental condition. I was becoming "average". The company's politics were affecting me too. Colleagues and friends turned their back and I involuntarily created enemies among my staff. Talking to my boss, meeting for performance reviews or presenting my work was very painful. I simply wanted to avoid all that.

After a while, I ended up losing the support of my team, my colleagues and managers. I had no future in there. I lost my job.

Although, it was never difficult for me to find another job, the situation repeated once again after a few months.

My mind was busy most of the time trying to find reasons or excuses. I thought my first employer did not give me the chance and opportunities to develop my full potential; I thought my second boss did not appreciate my talent; I thought my third boss was an insensible man and the following job simply was not the right one for me. The list of job experiences continued like that. In my mind, I was never in the right company, in the right industry or in the right role for me.

This feeling grew every day and it badly affected other areas of my personal life. My financial situation was deteriorating too. After many years of work, my balance sheet was in the red, no assets, no income and a lot of debts. I had worked hard but built nothing. My relationship with my family was not bad but it wasn't ideal either. I hardly had time to spend with my kids so I missed many days of their childhood and hadn't created strong family ties. I didn't have good friends or a social life and my spiritual life was somewhere near zero. I never realised that even my health was being affected by this situation. Poor results in each of these areas were a sad outcome after many years despite thinking I was doing successful and hard work.

With a family to look after, no job, no financial support and not knowing what to do next, I found myself completely lost, alone and scared. I did not know what I had done wrong. I did not know what I was missing, or what knowledge I did not have access to during my long career and education. I did not know how to get out of that situation I was in or how to react to it. Once again, fear, doubts, anxiety and worry was beating me.

I reviewed all the knowledge I had accumulated during my twenty-one years of education including my masters and a specialisation. I checked all the skills I had learned and developed. I looked at all the tools and techniques I had been given to sort out any problem I could face as a leader and nothing, absolutely nothing gave me a solution or even an answer to what was happening or what I needed to change in my life. So the most powerful weapon I had, the knowledge I got from my traditional education at top universities, simply did not work this time.

My critical turning point began in 2012 at the British Library. The answer to all my questions and the beginning of a new chapter in my life came from a couple of books. Although, they weren't "traditional leadership books", their great lessons were the beginning of a fantastic transformational journey that not only helped me to reclaim the life I was meant to live, but I also developed a clear mind with a strong purpose that have become the foundation of my authenticity and my personal and professional success.

After a few days of reading these books several times, learning from them and reflecting on their lessons, I became totally convinced I had to work on myself and condition my mind if I wanted to change my life. Nothing else would work. I recognised I had to put myself in a mental state where I needed to be at my best so I could ensure I had more of myself to give to my job, my staff, my company and my family. I understood that the first essential step to changing my results was to do inner work and change not only my mental attitude but my subconscious programming in order to be at my best. That idea was the one thing I could grab hold of to help me out of my difficult situation. What I did not know was the profound change it would bring to my life.

This really was new and special knowledge for me. I never read anything like this during my years of training as an industrial designer, marketing manager and as an MBA. From that moment on, I had what I like to call a gratifying personal transformation, not because I reached any higher spiritual state, but simply because I felt empowered to take on any adversity in my life no matter how hard it could feel. I now have a very specific state of mind and emotional strength, which orientates my conduct toward any external circumstance.

I began this conscious transformation journey (which really emerged out of being thrown out of my comfort zone) knowing that it would involve dramatic changes and being perfectly aware that there was a high probability of failure during this process this happened previously when I failed to make changes in my life. However, this time the result was different because I felt in control; it was all about me. I reflected on those previous experiences when I failed and felt frustrated and noticed that I had failed in all sorts of conditions. It did not matter what job I was doing, in what industry, with what people, not even what country I was living in, still I had failed. So clearly it wasn't the environment or the people around me that were affecting me. I was affecting myself.

My own mind was the only thing to blame for the kind of life I was living. Therefore, this time my transformation process started with the real source: my mindset. This time I challenged everything, I searched back from my childhood to the present and that was the beginning of the most powerful life transforming process that gave me extraordinary results in a relatively short time.

Only few days later, I decided to commit myself to this inner transformation, which involved a self-discovery and self-development process that took several months. A new sense of life and a completely new mental attitude emerged from the process of rediscovering myself, which resulted in true authenticity and personal success.

I began a lifelong process that continues day by day, hour by hour and even task by task, watching my thoughts consciously, studying and analysing them constantly, never surrendering, always learning from them, controlling them and making the right choice of thoughts, then mastering their application in the right way. I was at such a low level of consciousness and I never realised it. It took time and a lot of effort but the result is worthy.

It all occurs within ourselves. I learned that every new situation was an effect, so I kept linking it with the thought that caused it. I was doing it all the time and I appreciated I was also becoming patient and persistent. I grasped the feeling of obtaining self-knowledge, which is understanding, knowledge and power.

As a result, the quality of my life has improved tremendously in every dimension.

I have recognised, understood and clearly defined who I am. I accept, respect and value myself. I have built a strong character, which I am aware of and I enjoy expressing my personality in every word, in every action. This self-knowledge brought an extraordinary feeling of calm, freedom, emotion and positive energy that influence everything I do in my personal and professional life. I know who I want to become, I discovered my life purpose and I am living it day by day. The clarity of my purpose allows me to live purely focused towards its achievement.

This strong foundation and positive well-being of my personal life allows me to be more authentic when I am leading my team. I have a strong mindset that positively influences my attitude towards them and my work. As a result, my behaviour and actions have changed and are more focused towards the achievement of my professional goals, which are in line with my life purpose.

My mind is clear, I have a very positive mental attitude, I have better control over my thoughts and the way I react to any situation. Most of the time I am actively thinking and doing with my self-advancement in mind.

I have an increasing amount of energy that keeps me motivated and committed and an extraordinary inner force that helps me to keep on track and persevere even if things aren't going so well. I am more conscious of and enjoy the present, the now, and think less about the future. I have a whole new set of positive habits that help me to grow and open new doors for my personal development.

I have achieved the life balance I wanted, given priority to those areas I enjoy and care about the most, such as serving my family, serving others, being and developing myself and enjoying what I do. I am financially stronger than ever before, but more important, I have the time and the energy to spend with my children and my wife and live the life we want to live.

Every morning, every hour, every meal we have together is a moment that I consciously created since I was in the British Library and that's why it is easy for me to be consciously present during those moments we share together. The time I dedicate to work, I am fully present. I do not only enjoy it but I look forward to my working hours; I work in the environment I want to work, I have the schedule I designed according to my planned life, I work with the people I want to and it all makes me act in a certain way as my results are simply the results I expected to have. I do not hope to have good results anymore because I am confident that it will be the best result, the one I need in order to achieve my own life purpose.

I see life completely different from what it used to be, and, as a result, I have improved my financial life and have great potential to continue with this positive trend. I also have a very positive change in terms of my health and fitness. I am more conscious about my body and what it means to me. I value it more and look after it as never before. I appreciate, understand and use the power of my mind. I dedicate part of my time to study, learn and develop it and I am convinced I will do this for the rest of my life. I am clear and accept the "person-paradigm" that we are a body, mind and spirit and that I need to develop each of them in a balanced way if I want to enjoy true happiness.

As result of this personal development process, I also co-founded a company with my wife that allows us to work at what we like to do while helping others. The feeling of happiness when working in our business is indescribable. With passion and hard work, we have made it an international organisation that helps and supports leaders in Africa and Europe, by teaching and sharing with them the knowledge and experience we have gained during all these years. I was inspired and delighted to design three amazing courses that are inspirational to others and have been accredited by a respected organisation. We developed a partnership that helped us to achieve our dream of teaching and delivering our courses to many leaders in Africa who really needed this knowledge. My wife and I travel, work and we have fun, as enjoy what we do and, more important, we feel we're doing something that is meaningful and significant.

Obviously, I have many goals to achieve, including financial and personal goals; however, now I know that not achieving them does not define me. Recognising what I have achieved is a better way of living in my present with joy when I am on my way to achieve my definite purpose.

I wrote this book because I am convinced that the experience and knowledge I gained during the last thirty years can help those in executive, management or leadership positions to grow to their fullest potential in a way that is satisfying and enjoyable, rather than being on a difficult life journey. You can achieve this too if you commit to your personal development.

While I was going through these changes in my life, I was also very careful to understand and record, reflect and evaluate every step of my journey so I could one day confidently help those who are not necessarily career focused or in a leadership position, but were struggling with their personal life and wanted to find meaning in what they do to have a more fulfilling life.

You should read this book simply because it could immediately help you to improve the life you are living while making you a great human being. That is what our world need from all of us. This is what millions of other human beings need from you. This transformational journey will define a clear path for you and will produce the change that will help you to keep focused, make the right decisions, take actions and keep motivated to reach your full potential while helping to build a better world. I want to convince you that it is possible for you to develop to your fullest potential. Believe you can become more than who you are now, independent of your current situation in life.

Whatever your age, situation or condition, I know you probably feel this is going to be hard, that changing or doing something about it seems beyond your ability. Or maybe you feel you have too much to do, with too little time, and that important things are falling through the cracks and you don't even know what to do differently. You may have no idea how to start this. Know that you can always grow more and you have plenty of time to develop your potential. This is an incredible way to achieve it while living an amazing life and contributing to a better world.

In case you still have doubts about your possibilities, I also want to tell you that it is your responsibility as a human being to gain the force and enthusiasm to grow and develop your potential. Follow this idea of living a really complete and successful life and rise to the greatest possible height in talent. It will bring that amazing feeling of leaving your fingerprint and being significant to others.

Finally, with this journey, I feel like I have been awakened and my purpose now with this book is to show you how to become an authentic and successful person who leads others to greatness. It is my personal belief that only a few great leaders are needed to make a better world for all of us.

INTRODUCTION

In 2012, when flying to Nairobi from London to deliver one of my leadership development programmes, I was reading a McKinsey & Company report on leadership. Its findings showed that 89% of leaders and executives in 47 companies had average or below average performance. This is pretty much says that 9 out of 10 leaders had poor results and performance. They were simply not good enough!

Perhaps you have noticed that this result is not exclusive or limited to leaders or managers. Underperformance and poor professional achievement affects most people independent of their position, role, country or ethnicity. I myself went through it and underperformed for many years before I found the actual reason and a solution for why I was not achieving my goals. Why was I not achieving my goals? For many years, I asked the same question over and over again. In my rush to have an answer or reason for this problem, I was dragged to the wrong solution. I thought that the cause of my poor performance and all negative issues around me were either my lack of skill-set or the conditions of my working environment. It never occurred to me that the real cause of the problem was me; more specifically, my mindset. We tend to focus our energy on identifying reasons for the problem "out there" and we find it very hard to accept that the source of our external conditions (good or bad) is inside us.

But what is the actual problem we are talking about?

It is very important to define it because the lack of a clear understanding of the problem is what makes us arrive at the wrong solution. I will explain the real problem with a short story that happened in one of my speaking events in Lagos (Nigeria) in 2011. After my talk, one of the participants approached me and asked me to advise him about doing an MBA course in the UK in order to develop more skills and be promoted in his company. His other reason was that an international degree was culturally related to a high probability of a job promotion. After questioning his background, I learned that he already had two masters' degrees but he was not achieving his goals and found it hard to get promoted in his company. He blamed his boss, his role, his salary, colleagues and everything else around him for his situation. I asked him another set of questions and I learned from his answers that he already had the skills for the role. Still, his boss was constantly promoting other colleagues, the company was also paying higher salaries to others and his role and responsibilities were absolutely normal. Really there was nothing strange about his working environment. It was clear for me that his poor results had nothing to do with his skill-set or working conditions or the environment. It was all about him. The source of his problem was his mindset. His attitude and behaviour were influenced by the wrong mindset. His lack of self-confidence, vision, purpose and self-awareness as well as negative beliefs and thoughts were sabotaging him. I saw no need for him to have another degree, and recommended him to work hard on building the right mindset.

In spite of my advice, he still invested his time and money to pursue the MBA in the UK. Almost two years later I met him again. This time he was working for another company, and of course he was facing exactly the same issues. Unfortunately, he still believed that the problem was everything else, not him.

This is very common problem among all of us. I have taught and trained people in Africa, Europe and Latin America and I can tell you that the majority of us face this situation, regardless of our role or job position. Look at these three examples from some of my clients and you will find the same patterns or source.

This is what a young professional told me when we met first during training: "I have the potential and capabilities to grow professionally as a great leader, but people think I am not ready for it, and I am unprepared for the challenge and that is why most of the time I am unable to capitalise on opportunities for higher positions" (I am sure he meant "I do not feel ready for it and I feel fear).

Another junior manager replied, "Even though I have the formal education, the knowledge and the skills, I still lack of confidence and self-belief to lead others. When leading or managing others, I sometimes have doubts, anxiety, negativity and even anger. It negatively affects my day to day work, particularly the way I communicate."

Finally, one of the most senior in the group quietly agreed that sometimes the knowledge and the skills are not enough to succeed: "In my senior role, most of the time I feel overwhelmed with the ever increasing workload and pressure I face at work every day and became so obsessed with the return on invested capital and all other targets that I ended up becoming very short term in my thinking that I lost sight of the bigger picture and I do not feel I have full control of the situation. I permanently live in fear about our future, we live in fear of failure."

One area all of them have in common that refers to them as individuals and particularly to their mindset and their psychology. However, it is very difficult for us to recognise it as the real source of the problem. We do not know it, we are ignorant in this matter, and we suffer on a daily basis and live frustrated lives because of this ignorance. Clearly self-doubts, anxiety and fear did not allow these people to perform at their best and, as result, it was difficult for them to achieve good results. They were competing; they were anxious and scared of losing their position to others. Hence, they performed below average, just as the McKinsey & Company report indicated.

When we see underperformance as a result, we immediately think about enhancing performance through effective training with a skill-building approach, however, it doesn't last for long because as soon as we see we are making progress, we relax and return to old habits. We repeat this time and time again. Therefore, to make a real change, we have to look deeper and realise that it is the change in our mindset (our focus in this book) that can help us to improve this whole situation and make us truly successful.

16

The question you might be asking is, would it be possible for me to build or develop the right mindset, improve my performance and become who I really want to be? The answer is yes! And more than that, our goal here is to develop the right mindset to be authentic and successful individuals who aim to become great leaders.

This book will take you through a personal development process that helps you build the right mindset for you. This journey includes three stages. From these three stages, I created a three step process that will take you from where you are to the achievement of your definite personal vision that is significant for you and for others.

These three powerful steps are the structure of this book and it is my aim to explain them to you in a simple way you can easily follow to transform your life, then your personal leadership approach.

This is your journey to greatness.
START WORKING ON YOURSELF.

PART 1

BECOME AUTHENTIC

STEP 1. DISCOVER YOUR TRUE-SELF

Chapter. 1. This first step explains the foundation or basic knowledge you need in order to begin your transformational journey and create a strong desire to study yourself day and night.

Chapter. 2. It describes a legitimate process we can use to develop wisdom, to build character and cultivate a good heart. If followed correctly and fully, it creates the basis to think righteousness and always make the right decision, even if the outcome is not favourable for your own interest.

Chapter. 3. It illustrates the process to develop an incredible clarity about your high purpose, virtue and a crystal clear vision. This, in turn, will make you highly focused. It also explains the process how to have a more peaceful mind so you are able to speak, act and lead with a pure mind that is filled with great determination.

Chapter 1.

FOUNDATION

"He who in early days was unwise but later found wisdom, he illuminates this world like the moon when free from clouds".

-The Dhammapada.

BE THE CHANGE

"Another word for life is change.
Two words for suffering are resisting change"

-Michael Jeffreys

During my MBA, a good friend of mine was helping me with a project for the Change Management module. He was a consultant and expert on managing change; As he was working and supporting many large organisations primarily on policy and strategy changes, his knowledge about the change model, how to overcome barriers to change and how to ensure people accept and adapt and support the change was vast. However, he had the misconception that change was always external and mainly about others. When discussing changing ourselves and particularly changing himself, he found change extremely hard.

He was often stressed due to his job; he was suffering and so were his family. He complained that most people in his team were unprepared, so he had to do almost everything for them. Then he complained about his boss and the lack of support he got from him and even complained about having to deal with the worst customer who never followed instructions accurately. I asked him if he went to work every day with that mentality. Did he think that way about his colleagues and boss and customers every time he worked with them? Then I said to him, "With all those beliefs and thoughts in your mind when you are working, I am pretty sure your efficiency at work is not the best, is it?" It took him a while to understand that to improve his situation he was the one who had to change not the job, the company or the customers.

Following his knowledge, experience and skills, he began the process of change, but no matter how many times he tried, he always failed. He assessed his situation, planned multiple strategies, changed his behaviour and tried other methods that offered him a temporal change, though they never lasted. The expert change manager did not quite understand the key element of change. You cannot change habits or behaviour permanently if you do not involve your mind and start with your beliefs and your mindset.

Just like him, I had tried to change many things in my life, sometimes my career, sometimes the appearance of my body, my personality and many other aspects of my life, but I never succeeded. The changes were temporary, but for various reasons they never lasted and most of the time I came back to square one after few weeks. This is the classic example that happens to most of us with our New Year's resolutions. We plan the change, we implement it, change behaviours and after few weeks, we forget, we get bored and we simply stop doing it. Why? Although the desire for a change is there, in most cases, we do not feel capable of changing ourselves and when we feel able to change, we simply do not know how to do it successfully.

In your own case, you probably ask to yourself...how can I have a better life?...or better job, house or car? What should I do to become a better person? How can I change what I do for living? Those are important symptoms that indicate you are ready for a change, for a personal transformation process, but you first must ensure you are convinced that for your life to change you need to change first. If you want to have better opportunities, change yourself first. Do you want more friends, better relations, better employees, and better colleagues, change yourself.

Recognising we are the one who needs to change is the first step, but, in most cases, it never happens because we do not accept this and in the few cases that we accept it, then we do not even reach the next step. After your initial intention and even if you manage to begin the change, it does not last and you quickly come back to your original state or level.

The reason I am saying this is because I want you to be aware of the challenges you will face during this transformational journey from the very beginning. The need for change must be kept high at all times. We must motivate ourselves to initiate and continue the transformation process independent of any condition. It is easier to say than to do, so how can we do it?

The starting point for a permanent and successful change is to find your reason for change, your why; the bigger the reason is, the better it is for the process. So why do you want to change in the first place? Well, there are many possible reasons and the fact that you are reading this book clearly shows that you are looking for a change in your life, or at least that you are not entirely satisfied with your present condition.

We all want to improve or develop ourselves. It is part of our nature; we all want to fulfil our potential; we know there is more for us and continuously feel that something is missing even if we do not know exactly what it is. You have the right to enjoy an amazing life. Many people are truly living a great life...so why shouldn't you? Look at your present condition and think, is this all? Are you settling for the rest of your life?

After finding your why, the first battle to start a change process is against the belief that "you can't do it". Here we need to create hope and from there we must go further and create certainty. From this moment, we start working on our new mindset as we need to create that famous "CAN DO" attitude. You must build a new belief that will help you to get this positive mental state. The key is for you to believe and be convinced that your mind is already prepared with the necessary knowledge and energy to make the change and achieve your goal and it is your choice to accept it. I will explain this in more detail in chapter four, however, you will get a glance at this when you read next page. It all begins with a desire to be the change and the understanding and acceptance of two concepts: Greatness and Choice.

This is not a should, it's a must! You must believe in the power of your mind. I know it might be difficult for some of you to believe it since you do not have hard evidence but surely you sense it, you have the feeling that your consciousness might have some extraordinary powers that you have not tapped into yet. It is my intention to convince you first about this inner power and it is equally important to show you how to train your mind so you can condition it, and I will do this in great detail so that any potential question about this process will be answered in this book.

The reason I must convince you that to believe in this internal power is to believe in yourself is because it is the only way to give you the strength you need to transform yourself permanently. It is this conviction that produces a real and lasting change.

In the meantime, and until you have a better knowledge of this concept, please reflect and understand that as humans, we are constantly trying to achieve our full potential. And for that reason, we are constantly changing or at least have that permanent desire for a change or personal transformation. Change is necessary and it is good for us.

GREATNESS

"The greatness of a man is not in how much wealth he acquires, but in his integrity and his ability to affect those around him positively."

— Bob Marley

Greatness is the first foundational concept we must learn before starting our development journey. On the first floor of the British Library, in a quiet corner of the Business Centre room, a place where you can access almost any business, entrepreneurship and leadership book, journal, article or magazine ever published around the world, I found myself reading and learning about this extraordinary concept, which seems to be the conversion point for most great leaders: GREATNESS. This concept literally changed the way I think, my words and my actions.

Greatness is related to your infinite possibilities, it is accepting no limits to your potential; it raises your standards; you will never compromise the quality of your thoughts, words and actions and you will never settle for less than you deserve. It is a motivator that will keep you moving forward and expanding in all possible directions. When you take greatness as your principle, you immediately stop competing with anyone else. You are rising yourself to a higher level where you are committed to the highest achievement and to never stop working towards your personal development. It is simply a higher level of achievement and a clear understanding of this concept will make all your goals seem really small and achievable.

But how is greatness applied to our life, particularly to the way we can lead others?

I have dedicated the last 5 years to researching, learning and understanding how one can become a truly great leader. My drive has been the belief that only a handful of GREAT LEADERS is needed to change the world as we know it to the world we desire. It is only GREAT LEADERS who will be able to transform organisations, society, and reduce the suffering of humankind.

I read many books, hundreds of blog entries and articles, watched numerous videos and attended more conferences, including many of these being delivered by the most acknowledged scholars and university professors and many others by self-made leadership gurus and it strikes me as odd that there is vast difference in opinions and attitude on both sides about what makes a leader great. So, to give an answer to how one can become a Great Leader is not easy. However, as I believe that life is the best teacher, I will answer through the lessons I learned in real life from real people and through a long career in various fields.

I learned that great leaders understand who they really are at their core. They have the distinctive quality to perceive the right thing to do, the burning desire to serve others, which allows them to do the right thing! They are capable and strong enough to do the right thing due to their permanent effort to cultivate a good heart and develop wisdom. The essential foundation of greatness is wisdom, and great leaders have the wisdom to recognise the best ends to aim at and the best means for reaching those ends.

In his book "From Good to Great", Jim Collin introduced the concept of Level 5 leadership, which is related as the level of great leadership. He found that great leaders have humility, they don't seek success for their own glory, they're the first to accept blame for mistakes and they're fearless when it comes to making decisions. These are very special and admirable qualities, but do you see anything extraordinary in these qualities? If there is nothing super human in there, can we say that it is possible for any of us to become a great leader? Absolutely, why not? And this is the great lesson, you must first accept and believe that greatness is in you, it is in everyone of us; it is in each member of your family, it is in each friend, colleague, it is in each employee and each leader. This must be one of your core beliefs. It doesn't matter if you try to develop humility and discipline or take more responsibility and try to lead with passion. If you aspire to great leadership, you first have to accept and believe in your heart that there is greatness within you and see it in everyone else.

As for most of us, my personality was greatly influenced by the person closest to me in my early years: my mother. She always encouraged me to `THINK BIG` and to never be afraid of dreaming big, so I grew up with this feeling of always aiming for the highest possible level of success and I could not help immersing myself into the study of the science of being great. This immediately became an obsession for me when I realized GREATNESS was in EVERY person and you could grow in any direction you want as there does not appear to be any limit to the possibilities of personal growth! I was excited and terrified by this concept.

Shakespeare once wrote: `Be not afraid of greatness`. Well, I was certainly feeling afraid of greatness at first; I did not want to aim too high and then fail miserably, particularly during those days when I was at my lowest stage personally and professionally. However, I can tell you, the more you learn about this topic, the more you will feel that you can find greatness in yourself. To simply be open to greatness is to be aware and accept that you can improve yourself, your performance and your lives accepting no limits. You can truly become whoever you want to become and when you understand yourself, you can create your own destiny. From now on, continuously read and learn about greatness. Listen to audio recordings and watch as many talks and interviews with great people and any other videos related to greatness. Dedicate a few minutes every day to this activity. Switch off the TV and start filling your mind with this knowledge and be prepared to see and feel the first change in your belief system.

Once you accept greatness is within you and you aim for it, you won't tolerate being around people who make you aspire to anything less.

CHOICE

"But until a person can say deeply and honestly, 'I am what I am today because of the choices I made yesterday,' that person cannot say, 'I choose otherwise.'"

-Stephen R. Covey

"Choice" is the magic word. It can change everything in a second. It is true power; it makes you conscious of the control you have over your selections, decisions and your reactions to external situations or conditions.

Choice of attitude.

A couple of years ago, one of my colleagues, a professor with a PhD and lifelong Buddhist tradition and beliefs, was upset with me because I disagreed with him about one of his academic decisions. Before that situation, he used to be a good friend of mine, who complimented my leadership style and constantly encouraged me to continue pursuing my professional goals. However, after our disagreement, he felt really offended and allowed his frustration to take control of him. He started to insult me in front of my team and other colleagues. That frustration became anger and it was so bad that he tried to humiliate me by ridiculing my leadership approach, my academic credentials and my personality; While the situation was very challenging and perhaps my staff expected me to react strongly and use my "power" as his manager, I chose to keep a peaceful mind and consciously remained calm. Even though he was insulting me in front of other managers and shouted offensive words in the corridors and offices of our company, I consciously chose to feel compassion for him; I understood his frustration and his suffering. This decision immediately raised me to a superior mental level. I quickly became aware of his emotions and did not allow them to influence my state of mind and affect my behaviour.

I took control of the situation. I answered him with carefully selected kind words and it was all resolved. It was incredible the respect I gained after that day; not only my team but every staff member complimented my mental ability to endure abuse in peace.

A couple of days later, he recognised his mistake and even though he never apologised for the incident he told me something much better. He told me he would like to know how I was able to keep my mind, words and body under self-control with only a couple of years of practicing meditation, training the mind and reading Buddhist philosophy and that he could not, despite being a Buddhist his whole life. I told him I truly understood the power of "choice".

It is true that we cannot always choose the things around us but we can ALWAYS choose how we react to those things. Being able to consciously choose how we will react to any situation in a normal day every time is a big step to live in harmony, cultivate a great heart and a well guarded mind. But that's not all. What I really want you to realise is that CHOICE is not just how you react to situations in terms of your feelings, but more than that, it is how you approach your life as a whole.

Choice in life.

You might or might have not realised that you have been living in reaction to the demands of others; to the demands of the world. I first heard this in a conference and it really caught my attention. Every day you wake up and immediately fall into the race of "what needs to be done urgently", your day is pretty much set for you already. You look at your emails and react to them then you check social media and react to whatever is there, the same with the demands of your work and your friends and family. We think we are in control because we have plan, an agenda for our day, but what we do not realise is that every single item on the agenda is a reaction to something or someone. We are so used to it. This is how we deal with life and the way we will continue living if we do not realise that we have a choice. What a mistake! It's like going to the cinema, not knowing you can choose the movie you want to watch, then you buy the ticket not knowing what movie you are going to watch, sit in there and just wait to see what film will be showed to you. This is really what happens to most of us.

Here I ask you, are you reacting to life instead of living it proactively? In my case, I realised I was being controlled by circumstances. I used to believe that my destiny was decided by external factors. I was shocked to realise I was, just as Wallace D. Wattles described, "the child of chance and circumstance and the slave of fear" - nothing else. I realised that most of us wake up every day passively waiting to see what the day has for us rather than consciously choosing what you want out of your day. this is "living life on your own terms".

Abraham Lincoln, Mahatma Ghandi, Charles de Gaulle and many others knew that the choices they had in life were always about themselves (and their reactions) and never about the external factors around them. (Big lesson!)

Realising that you have a choice is to primarily stop reacting to whatever comes to us and proactively creating the experiences we want to have during our day. To have a day full of great moments, before I do anything at all, I condition my mind. I dedicate an instant to knowing how I want to feel that day; I imagine how it is going to feel then I "feel" it first and with that clarity, I focus on the best of each experience and I remain alert of any negative thoughts that could affect the way I want to feel.

With this morning routine, you will never again hope things will go the way you want, your mind will be consciously seeking that things happen the way you want them to. You must feel in total control of yourself and your future. You must believe that it is your choice: to keep reacting or to change completely. It is not easy but it is very important that you make the effort to do it.

With this knowledge, I began organising my day in a different way. As much as I could, I created my day the way I wanted it to be, I chose the activities I truly wanted to do, and even though I was working for someone else and had an agreed schedule, I chose the attitude I wanted to have towards my work and how I would do it.

Choice on Decision-Making

Life is a matter of choice and our current condition is the result of our choices or decisions. Look at your current situation right now and realise that it is the result of your previous choice. Do the exercise: see your current situation, track it back and you will find out it was your choice. I know your "logical mind" might try to convince you that this is not always true or at least is not true in your case, but ignore it and continue seeking. To make it easier for your mind to accept it, start by blaming yourself and try looking for evidence that you are right and that you are responsible and the one to blame for the choice. Track it back and you will find it was your decision, your choice.

A clear understanding of the concept of choice will put us in a completely different position or perspective when making any decision. It brings us to the present moment before we make the decision. Being in the present moment makes us aware of our feelings and emotions which can influence our decisions. It also makes us conscious of our responsibility for the outcome of that decision. This is extremely important as many times we make the wrong decision as we are influenced by how we are feeling the moment we made the decision.

Every moment of the day when I am making a decision, I consciously know I am creating my future and whether good or bad, I know it will be my responsibility, so I want to be sure I am perfectly aware of how I feel and what my predominant emotion is when making decisions.

So far, this is all theory and no change will happen if you do not put this into practice. To maximise the use of the power of choice, it is essential to embed this idea in your new and growing mindset. Life does not happen to me, it happens for me. This should be your state of mind at all times if you want to stop reacting and start creating the life you want to live.

This is a fundamental statement, and after having all the necessary data and reflecting on it, I reached my decision and chose to believe it. From that moment, I accepted and never questioned it again. I created this state of mind by repetition and autosuggestion

(I will discuss this in the second part of this book). I cannot tell you how many times I repeated this statement in my mind over and over. Soon I realised that it was helping me to approach daily situations in a different way and of course I was seeing different results.

My decisions, the simple and the complex, as well as my actions had to go through this new concept in order to be approved or rejected. It was slowly giving me a new sense of control over my behaviour and actions.

After I learned about the concept of choice, and I heard about it in different audiobooks as well as some particular videos, I became totally convinced in my heart and in my mind that it was entirely up to me to continue living my life as an average person or to make a drastic CHANGE in my life and become that person I was meant to be.

Keep reading every day and listening to as much as you can about the power of choice until you feel you are fully convinced you understand this and are ready to apply it. Soon it will start influencing your attitude and your behaviour, at least every time you are making a decision. It is extremely important as the foundation of your personal development. For a wise person, every thought, every word and every action will always come after the careful and natural use of the concept of the power of choice.

THE CLEAR-MINDED LEADER

*"If you correct your mind, the rest
of your life will fall into place."*

-Lao Tzu.

So far, I have referred to "Great Leaders", "Authentic Leaders" and the idea of an "Authentic Person" as the foundation of both of them. However, behind any of these labels is one common element, a clear mind!. Authentic and successful leaders are clear-minded leaders.

Therefore, it is important for me to define what a clear-minded leader is before we begin the teaching of how to become one.

A clear-minded leader represents the idea of someone who has a particular way of thinking, a particular attitude and way of behaving and acting as a result of a self-trained and strong mindset and is continuously improving. I define "the clear-minded leader" as someone who has three definite elements that give them supreme self-control over their mind, words and body: (1) a crystal clear understanding of their true self; (2) a well-guarded mind; and (3) an extraordinary source of energy.

These are the three elements that certainly will make a leader truly authentic from inside out, with a clear high purpose, a definite goal and a mind filled with energy and the determination to achieve it. These are also the three vital elements for success.

This book is organised around these three topics and each chapter discusses the beliefs and principles as well as the techniques that need to be used in order to become a clear-minded leader.

(1) A crystal clear understanding of the true-self

This is the result of a long and constant inner work that involves the desire to study yourself day and night by going deeply into your subconscious mind to understand your beliefs to stop any resistance towards yourself and begin to accept who you truly are. With constant practice, you will become more self-aware and confident when expressing your personality; you will cultivate a good heart, which will be reflected in better people and relationship management, but more important, you will balance self-interest and the common good. In other words, you are building up your emotional intelligence and you are developing wisdom.

(2) A well-guarded mind

This is the second component needed in order to protect the new self-knowledge you acquired. Build a vigilant watchfulness mind that is alert and ready to control any sign of worry, doubt, anxiety or fear. This is the process that maintains a peaceful state of mind that gives the leader a strong level of attention, concentration and effective decision-making.

With constant effort, you will (subconsciously) develop powerful positive thinking and a positive attitude, which is one of the qualities that will increase your ability to influence others.

During this step, you are working towards gaining supreme self-control, where you are able to control the anger of the mind, word and body, think righteously and be able to speak and act with a pure mind.

(3) An extraordinary source of energy

When you have made some progress towards the ability to keep your mind and body under self-control, you are now ready to think and act harmoniously, balanced and effectively, thus, the key is the development of will power to act! Not only to work rightly as a great leader, but to live in joy while you are confident you will achieve your definite purpose.

THE WHOLE-PERSON PARADIGM BALANCE PHILOSOPHY

"As a rule, the mind, residing in a body that has become weakened by pampering, is also weak, and where there is no strength of mind there can be no strength of soul."

-Mahatma Gandhi

I am pretty sure you have a friend or you know someone who is very concerned about his or her physical appearance and is always in the gym working out or trying a new diet to lose weight. Some of them are constantly looking at themselves in the mirror, constantly checking if their hairstyle is the right way, if makeup is perfect and, of course, taking selfies every 10 seconds and posting them on their social media so they can get the expected complements. On the other hand, you might know a person who is completely different, who never cares about their appearance but is totally submerged in books and intellectual activities For them, it doesn't matter how their body looks or what they eat or anything related to their external appearance. In fact, they do not care about any of that at all.

These two people have a body and a mind, but they are giving different preferences to one over the other. They have focused and developed one area much more than the other, hence they have denied the other area to develop at the same level.

It is very important to understand that you as an individual recognise and deeply accept that we are not just our body; the self also involves the mind, the soul and the heart.

The lesson I learned from a resident monk in one of the London Meditation centres was to live for these four motives: body, mind, soul and heart. This is exactly what the leadership guru Steven Covey described as the "Whole-Person Paradigm". Moreover, none of these elements of the self is more important than the other and as Wallace D. Wattles wrote, no one of them can live fully if either of the others is cut short of full life and expression.

Of this we must be convinced. We cannot simply try to accept it at a mental level, it is fundamental for our transformation process to believe with our whole heart and mind that this is the only truth.

Most of the self-help books from beginning of the 20th century talk about this constantly, so I read as many of these books as I could in order to first understand the principle and its roots and then to be fully convinced about this magnificent truth.

I was finding it hard to accept it and even harder to fully believe I am more than my body. In fact, it took me a while to truly understand this concept or revelation and it was in the middle of a meditation and spiritual retreat that I realised how true it is. I was on the second day of meditation, and though the two days had been amazing for my mental and spiritual growth, I fell ill, and as much as I tried to continue the meditation and the learning process, I physically was not able. My body became very weak and I was losing concentration, attention and focus. I realised how much I depended on a strong and healthy body to successfully develop the other areas of myself.

After this lesson, I learned that my personal development and daily routine would not be complete if I didn't include activities for the development each of these areas. The scope of this book is limited only to the training and development of the mind and does not include the body; however, I would like to mention that to live fully, I take great care of my body. I primarily ensure I get good sleep and I make sure I start every day (first thing in the morning) with one or two glasses of pure water, five minutes of breathing exercise (Pranayama or the breath of life), good food and a bit of recreation or exercise. I will expand more in my morning routine in the second part of the book.

Why is this so important?
When I began reflecting and meditating on the idea of myself

being more than just my body, I first felt that it triggered an stoppable willingness and interest to find out who I truly was.

I became increasingly aware of a need for self-discovery. The question 'who am I' was the origin of my journey to finding my authentic self. It gave me a new purpose, a real, fundamental purpose in my life. Clearly, it was a unique way for me to become truly an authentic person and the base for authentic leadership.

It also gives real meaning to the concept of greatness. Even if the body has some limitations, our mind, heart and spirit know no limits. This is the concept that opens a whole new and unknown world to our extraordinary human powers and as a result we gain a strong desire and aspiration to discover and conquer those powers.

Understanding the person paradigm also made it much easier for me to shift from resistance to acceptance of my physical appearance as it was just one part of myself and never the only element that defined me.

How does it feel to know that you are more than your body and your face?
I personally believe it is extremely important in order to be authentic and successful since much of our confidence is based on how we see our body (self-image) and how we think others see us, believing this is ourselves. This is the authentic and fastest way to build self-confidence. I realised my heart, my mind and my spiritual side have tremendous value. I value them so much! Now I truly value myself! I finally learnt to value who I am. I was able to see how my self-belief was soaring day-by-day and others start noticing it too.

The result of accepting and valuing your being as the whole-person is that as much as you recognise yourself, you start recognising others in the same way. You will see your family, your partner, your children, your colleagues and friends in a completely different way. I recognised how wrong we are when we define someone by what we see, just the physical part. It is, of course, a more spiritual way that helps you to avoid the habit of judging others by their appearance.

Note that at a mental level, you have the belief that you do not judge people by their appearance, but this does not always happen and we end up judging not only people but situation or conditions.

Seeing people and understanding them for who they really are was one of the first and biggest steps I took in transforming myself not only as a person but also as a leader. Very soon my team and colleagues realised how much I started valuing them truly as human beings, recognising them not for what they did or what they have but purely for who they were. Can you imagine how this value increased my ability to influence others? As a person and as a leader, I realised I was communicating more effectively than ever before. No matter how many courses I did before, the result was never as good as how I started relating to others when I clearly understood this concept.

In terms of personal development and growth, I set my mind and valued the integral and balanced development of the mind, the body, the soul and the heart as the way to complete human expression.

I created a set of developmental targets for each of these areas. I dedicated some time to think and visualise what I wanted to achieve with my body physically, what I wanted to achieve mentally, spiritually and in my heart. This influenced my attitude and habits. Now my focus was in each of those areas, developing them in everyday activities. I balanced my personal growth time every day and distributed it among activities that could help me to develop all the areas.

I started talking about the person paradigm to my family, my children and to everyone else. I include it as a topic in all my lectures so I constantly had the idea in my mind to embrace it and make it a firm belief. From there it was relatively easy to develop great habits. I consciously and effortlessly began meditating and taking some time for pure thinking and reflection, and I also looked at improving my diet and physical exercise. It became my life purpose to fully develop myself in all these areas and I began organising my whole life around it.

ADDICTED TO SELF-LEARNING

"The best of men are self-trained men,
those who can endure abuse in peace".

-The Dharmapath

Personal development, particularly self-development, is the one activity you must focus in order to improve everything else in your life. The reason is that when we work on our self, we are not looking at obtaining external knowledge, as we focus purely on the growth of one's personal self and we do this with the primary aim of self-fulfilment and proactively reaching our fullest potential. Please read this statement again because you need to understand how important self-development is in your life.

Self-development is the path to grow and the path to live a real life as you are focused on expressing your full potential in terms of body, mind, soul and heart every day. Use self-development as a lifelong process that keep you changing and improving to become the person you want to be and to reach true happiness in life.

Get convinced of this: the purpose of your life must be essentially development, personal growth and fulfilment. This is a belief that needs to be embedded in our mind, your soul and your heart. This can be your greatest motivation that will keep you making a continuous effort to develop your abilities to become the person you are meant to be.

You have the possibility to rise to your greatest possible height in talent and full potential no matter what your current situation is now. You only need to make the decision. Many people achieve their goal because they consciously decide to prioritise their personal growth over anything else. Realise that all you need, the greatest tools and powers, is inside you and available for you.

41

Make use of them.

I have read several ancient Asian books as well as modern literature on personal development and they all mention and agree on one essential idea: "The object of all life is development; the purpose of nature is the advancement and unfolding of life; Therefore, everything that lives has an inalienable right to all the development it is capable of attaining." If you look for anything alive in the universe, you will see it. Isn't that amazing? Your desire to realize your innate possibilities is inherent in your human nature. I am saying this to convince you that failing to consider continuous personal-development is clearly against the purpose of nature. Use your time to develop your ability, focus on becoming the best you can be.

In a world where change is constant, you need to change or you will be changed. Staying in the same place where you have been for years and doing the same thing you have been doing for years would keep you in the same situation and will never take you to the place you want to be.

In 2012, I made personal growth and continuous self-development a part of my mindset, and since then I have worked harder to become the person I want to be. The great advantage of self-development is that I have customised my training strictly to my personal needs. I have designed a plan that focuses primarily on developing the abilities in those ideas that could help me to accelerate my career or make me healthier, financially independent and spiritually stronger. The motivation is to develop abilities that help me to become the person I want to be.

With this, you are ready to start your self-development journey. Remember that you are engaging in a completely new way of life that involves continuous mental conditioning and habit creation for the rest of your life. These two will become your habits from some other strong beliefs. The process, as mentioned before, involves three steps, self-discovery, self-control and self-mastery.

Before you continue, I would like to warn you that the whole process starts with having an open mind. This is absolutely necessary as we will have to break most of the rules we have been governed by. We will challenge every single idea, concept, old belief and suggestions that come from us or from someone else. You are to listen primarily to your inner self. Everything that you have learned so far is subject to reconsideration. If you are ready for it, then it will all be very natural, but if you aren't open minded, you will face hard times trying to be convinced of anything that goes against what you currently know as reality or common sense. Remember, *"He who would attain highly must sacrifice greatly."*

Chapter 2.

WHAT ARE YOU MADE OF?

"Knowing yourself is the beginning of all wisdom."

— Aristotle

SELF-DISCOVERY:
FINDING YOUR TRUE SELF

"Discovering who you are today is the first step
to being who you will be tomorrow"

-Destiny's Odyssey

CEO, directors and managers come to my Authentic Leadership courses and seminars with questions about building trust and motivating people (two fundamental areas for a leader). How do I build trust? How can I motivate my team? These are two of the most frequent questions asked by junior and senior managers, and most of the time they expect a quick fix answer, a toolset, a new strategy or at least an idea to change their habits in order to improve results or performance in these two areas.

The general expectation is an external solution, something out there that could help them to get the results. However, during the course, they learn that building a strong mindset with a clear purpose, a virtue and vision is the key concept and foundation of trust. Cultivating a good heart and developing a positive mental attitude is the real solution to building strong relations based on trust. It allows you to think, speak and act with a pure mind.

Knowing who you are, where you want to go or who you want to become is the endless self-motivator for you, and the energy that truly influences and motivates other people to follow. This can only be achieved by immersing ourselves in a self-discovery journey that aims at finding our true-self. The best you can ever do is to know yourself. Any external skill or technique is just a short-cut, a temporal solution that does not create trust or inspire people.

During my leadership course, we start with an ice-breaking

exercise. Participants have to introduce themselves without mentioning their job title or their professional background. This simple exercise has proved to be very challenging for them. Junior and senior managers feel ashamed and unable to give a detailed answer. They are not prepared, they are not aware, they really do not know who they truly are. In most cases, it goes like this, "I am..." and they continue with their names and position... "I am the managing director of..." They get shocked when I make them realise that that their name is just a label to identify them but that is not who they are, their profession is only their role, just what they do, but that isn't who they are. Some of them become frustrated to discover they aren't clear about this essential question.

With this lack of self-knowledge, no wonder many leaders do not connect with their own team. How can they possibly get to know and sincerely understand their team when they do not know their true self? Without self-knowledge, it is harder to inspire credibility and without credibility, it is very challenging to influence others.

On the other hand, in relation to motivation, it is very hard to try to motivate someone if you yourself do not feel motivated. It is the knowledge of where we want to go, the clarity of a definite goal or the purpose to achieve a vision that would naturally motivate us and fill us with the energy and determination to achieve it. Only with this clear knowledge and certainty of knowing where we are going can we confidently motivate others to follow us. Without this knowledge it is hard for a leader to relate to his/her organisation and connect to its vision and even harder to influence and convince followers. How can they passionately relate and live their corporate vision or mission when they do not even have their own personal vision? They can't. Think about this, how could you ever align yourself as an individual with your organisation's purpose when you simply are not clear about your own purpose and where are you heading?

Without self-knowledge of who we are and who we want to become, it is very difficult to connect to others at personal and professional level, making it harder to build trust and inspire action.

With that consideration, would you expect from you or any of your team members high performance, efficiency, motivation and great results? Would you expect authenticity and success? It simply would not happen as each of them are first the result of an inner work, a self-discovery journey.

My self-discovery journey began with self-awareness and it led me to an ever-growing self-knowledge. The definite aim in this part of the development is supreme self-knowledge.

Self-awareness should be then your starting point and the main focus or the key idea is to answer the two (possibly) most important questions in your life: Who you are and who you want to become.

Finding clear answers for those two questions is truly the gate of wisdom. The first question (Who am I) will join you with your true-self and will give you authenticity. Here, the goal is more about understanding and self-acceptance by identifying, analysing and evaluating your beliefs, thoughts, feelings and emotions and to develop the power to manage and control them.

The second question (Who I want to become) will set your original path to live your purpose and define your personal vision. The key here is to build the mindset behind a strong mental attitude to never give up. That will keep us on track particularly when facing adversity. We must look to our talents, traits and qualities and see their relation with those activities that we love to do as well as the things we value most in our lives. All this knowledge helps us to develop passion for who we are and what we do and to make the right decisions and consciously choose the right path to live a fulfilling life.

This combination is the most powerful way to focus your whole life towards the achievement of your purpose. Having this clarity and this focus in your life are fundamental qualities you must have before you attempt, commit or take the responsibility to lead someone else. This is a vital preparation for leaders to make comfortable decisions, even in the face of ambiguity.

In the next couple of chapters, I will explain in detail the way I started this process and what really needs to be done to answer these two questions in the right way. This is a simple process but not easy. You cannot force it, you have to be patient with yourself. You need a lot of willpower, energy and time to dedicate to it. I wasn't looking for something special. In fact, at that moment in time, I didn't think I could have anything special to offer. I was basically looking for something but I wasn't sure what. Fortunately, the more I searched, the more I found out about me. Do not have big expectations, just do the work and appreciate what you find. This is all an essential part to be authentic and a key element for success.

I didn't escape to a faraway place in order to do this exercise. I didn't lock myself in a hotel room to do to be able to concentrate. I simply chose to have more time with myself. I allowed this time for me and let myself go deep in thinking and reflection, particularly about my feelings and my emotions, preferences, values and beliefs as well as doubts and fears.

This is the moment when you really begin to focus on discovering "who you are". When you do this constantly and it becomes a habit, you start knowing yourself better, understanding your purpose in life and clarifying the core principles on which you base your actions and behaviour. You are moving from what you thought you were to who you really are. That is an amazing experience that feels as if you're meeting who you truly are again.

It is very important that you record all these self-discovery activities. To support my self-learning I created a file called "Who am I?" and I was writing all my experiences, without any particular order, reason or preference. I did this exercise consistently every day. This document is extremely valuable and you will find yourself revisiting it constantly as it will become a strong motivator and a source of energy.

Spending some hours writing about yourself is perhaps the difficult part at this stage, when you see everyone else doing normal stuff and feel life is passing and you are there writing "nonsense" about yourself. This is the time you need your willpower, the commitment and the courage not to give up on this exercise. Why? Because everything, absolutely everything, will be against it, against you.

However, the worst enemy is your own conscious mind. It will attack you in every possible way; it tells you, this is a waste of time, there is no way out of it, forget about all this and stick to having a normal life just like anyone else; it will create all sorts of doubts and fear as it thinks in a logical way.

But if you are devote time to this exercise and you do it on a daily basis with full intention, you will start noticing some changes in yourself, even if you do not find big answers at the beginning. It is not that you are changing, it is that you are now finding yourself. Because you have dedicated time purely to yourself, you will naturally feel you start valuing yourself more.

I also want to make it clear to you that the self-discovery process I went through is not what we normally think it is. Some sessions have many tests, questionnaires that will take you in detail through a large number of concepts such as values, character and personal characteristics and you will have to dedicate some time to reflect, think and explore yourself and answer those questions to help you to identify many hidden traits, talents, strengths and weaknesses that you have.

These exercises alone won't make any difference, but don't get me wrong, these questionnaires are very important and definitely we need to do them; however, the self-discovery process is itself a way of living. It is dynamic. You are constantly exploring and discovering your true-self minute by minute, in every action you do during your normal day. It is a constant self-awareness in every activity. This is the key and this is what makes the difference. To be able to do this, you first need the ability of being consciously aware of the present situation as well as your actions and your reactions to it. This is an amazing ability and not easy as it takes time, but it is possible to acquire and it is worthy. It is not only possible, but we actually need it in order to have control over our emotions.

When I am having a conversation with someone, it is like having a full-body mirror next to you where your image in the mirror is observing all your physical expressions, paying full attention to your emotions, attitudes and reactions to the conversation and is concentrated on that unique moment only.

51

But be careful not to misunderstand this and think you are very aware when you are in a conversation. When other person is talking and you are mentally evaluating everything and preparing the "right" answer for them, you falsely believe you are being fully aware and in control of the situation. Nothing is further from the truth. This is a selfish action because your mind is not there, it is far away finding reasons, excuses, or arguments to create your answer to impress them. Opposite to that, what we want is to be consciously aware of ourselves in that particular situation, so we learn and understand ourselves and the way we interact with others.

Of course, at a conscious level, self-discovery makes sense and surely you agree with it. However, you and me know that this is not enough to make us take real action towards the understanding of ourselves; So, the first thing we need to work on is developing a strong desire to do it, to really commit to it. We need to develop willpower to take the first step. This is the key element of the whole process. I will explain in part three how this can be achieved. So here I should remind you to read this book fully first and then you can come back and start working on it chapter by chapter.

As William Ganson stated, "The inclination to know yourself rarely become strong until it hurts your pride or your pocketbook" and this is absolutely true but it does not need to be like that. You can also do it before going through any pain if you choose to develop your full potential and follow your life purpose but you need nerve, a lot of effort and patience to develop a strong desire to study yourself day and night.

As you can see, the idea of self-discovery for me was simply a search for knowledge about my inner self in a positive way, while accepting all my negative qualities and others' negative feedback during the process with a humble mind. Once you become acquainted with your true qualities (and provided you have the ambition), you can then improve each of these qualities. However, this is not the goal of this personal growth process; we are not working to improve bad qualities, but rather to strengthen our good ones so we can grow. This gives us the basis of where to start, and highlights the really good things about you!

Whatever your current situation in life is, the suggestion here is that you start easily by observing and paying more attention to those qualities that you have, those areas, actions or activities that you truly love to do or that make you feel joy every day and for as long as you can keep your concentration on what you value the most. Truly, this was my starting point, the origin of the first idea about my company and the way I wanted to live the second half of my life. As Napoleon Hill wrote: "One sound idea is all you need to achieve success." I would like to add that this is the only place where a true "sound idea" can come out for you. For me, since that moment, this is the place I look for opportunities that are perfect only for me. This exercise will be very useful for the next stage when we will be exploring our life purpose. It is all related to the new vision you will craft, the life planning you will develop and the goals you want to achieve.

With time, you will realise you have developed an extraordinary quality that is not only important for any person, but is fundamental for someone who is leading a team. It is balancing the needs of self and others in one's everyday life and, as a result, developing compassion, non-defensive self-awareness, and interdependent self-identity. At the end of these converging paths lies our **true self**, who is less concerned with self-promotion than with the flourishing of both the self and others. This is how you begin cultivating a good heart and a pure mind that will enable you to think, speak and act in righteousness.

It is my dream that all our leaders act on this and find their true self and, with a good heart and a pure mind, lead others in this path.

For free resources including my TOP 20 Self-discovery questions, please contact me or register at www.theclearmindedleader.com

TIME TO THINK OR THINKING YOU DON'T HAVE TIME

"Time is a created thing. To say 'I don't have time,'
is like saying, 'I don't want to.'"

-Lao Tzu

For you, the most important person in the world is and should be you. For that reason, you need to dedicate time to yourself, not just in how you do things but mainly to think about yourself. Most of us never dedicate a few minutes to think about ourselves even though a few minutes of pure thinking has tremendous benefits to our lives.

Dedicating a sacred time every day to sit down for at least ten minutes with full attention and concentration can give so much clarity to your mind that even your biggest problems seem to have an easier solution. It is incredible, as no one knows your problems and their solutions better than your inner self. Unfortunately, we do not tap into it. Every time we have a problem, we can be sure that we already know what the solution is. We just need to allow and give the mind a conscious time to unfold the answers for you.

As an individual, and much more as leaders, we keep ourselves very busy, doing several things at the same time. As our mind is permanently at work trying to cope with every task, every email, every call, we think we are using it effectively and efficiently; We sort out our problems when we drive, when we are in a conversation, when we are eating, we are thinking about the solutions to our problems, but rarely do we give our mind a fully dedicated time to think in a focused way.

Sitting on a chair for twenty minutes with full attention and concentration on the task of thinking is never a waste of time. In fact, it can be one of the most productive activities of the day. As I have what is now called "a large family" (three kids), me and my wife were permanently on the move, always in a rush, with not a single minute of the day to stop and think. We were working, studying our masters and taking care of the children's academic and non-academic activities. Since early in the morning, we rushed to get ready and try to be on time for everything, so we simply did not have time to think. We lived like that for many months, we left a lot of things incomplete, missed things, made wrong decisions and on top of that, every day we ended up exhausted and with the frustration that the following day would be the same. We lost clarity of our main goals, we didn't have time to think about our feelings, our moods and our purpose. The more things we did, the worse it was for us because our actions were becoming inefficient.

The time came when my personal development journey demanded more time of me to think, to think about myself. I learned to do things the way I wanted to do them by dedicating time to think. I needed to develop the ability to keep my attention and concentration on the thoughts I wanted to have so I could act accordingly. Thus, I made a conscious decision to allow time to myself, to take few minutes out of every day to think purposely. This "thinking" time paid off! In just a few days, I felt the clarity of where I was going with my life again. I got off that "permanent rush-hour" simply by focusing on those activities that were a priority in relation to my personal and family vision. I ensured I was doing fewer activities, though each and every single activity was done more efficiently. Filling our days with fewer activities done efficiently creates successful days.

We think about everything from the moment we open our eyes early in the morning. We always have the problems, the issues, the targets, the friends, the meetings, etc. on our mind all the time. This is a distracted mind but still, if anyone ask us if we dedicate time to think, most of the time and with full confidence we answer yes, but this is not the best use of this faculty.

We spend our time keeping ourselves busy for the whole day, but we do not take five minutes to think about ourselves. This seems to be a universal phenomenon.

In September 2013, I began training a large group of mature people originally from Eastern Europe. They were very experienced and educated people, thus they were very confident about their knowledge in different matters. They actively engaged in political, economical or social discussions based on what they read or watched, but they had literally no knowledge, no idea about their personal purpose in life. They were not clear about what their definite goal in life was and had absolutely no clarity about where they were heading with their life. They rarely thought about it; when I asked them how much time they were spending every day to purely think about their vision, or what they were working for every day, or who they were planning to become, nearly all of them realised they spent no time thinking about themselves. They had no time, not even five minutes a day to at least make sense of where they are heading with their lives. I do not blame them; most people are walking in darkness even though we all carry a light within.

We all live with the illusion of having less time so we need to live in a hurry, but if you do not have a clear and definite aim to live towards before you die, then what are you racing against in your life?

I asked this group of students, and perhaps you can ask these questions to yourself,

- If you do not know your life purpose and you do not know where you are going with your life, then why are you rushing?
- Why are you so busy if you are not building anything towards a definite goal?
- Is it your purpose to keep busy and running around until the day you die?

Without a definite goal, aim or vision, time is just an illusion. I don't think we have less or more time, time simply is. In fact, without a definite vision, you shouldn't even say "I am wasting my time" Why? If you are heading nowhere; how can you waste time?

You will arrive nowhere if you do not know where you are going, and you won't know where you are going if you do not dedicate time to yourself, time to think.

Dedicate a few minutes every day purely to think about yourself. Fully concentrate on yourself. This must become a habit. I made it a habit when I convinced myself that I had been living with my own body, mind, soul and heart for nearly forty years and I did not know it. I made the commitment to sit down and concentrate my thoughts for twenty minutes every day, to think about who I was, what I wanted to achieve or the person I intend to become. By doing it consistently, you will also start the unfolding your own deepest being and forming an image of this person.

Dedicating a daily time to think also made me realise the real reasons why I wasn't achieving any success and why I wasn't enjoying my personal and professional life as I should. For instance, thinking about myself made me realise that I always look at the "big picture" first, then move into tasks and details. I am more of a visionary person with long-term goals and a lot of determination to see a vision become reality. That is my drive, that is my motivation, but in reality, I was in a role that would not allow me to demonstrate the best of my capabilities. In fact, this role required the opposite; I needed to be very detail oriented and focused on implementing small tasks, without quite understanding the purpose or the bigger aim. This sort of situation at work can bring you or your staff frustration, lack of motivation, low performance and even destroy your confidence. Here fall the millions of people including managers and leaders who are working or doing something that they are not good at or, even worse, that they do not want to do.

Dedicate at least fifteen minutes every day until you are very clear about who you are, what you want to do and what you are good at but also what you cannot and should not be doing. After that, your fifteen minutes should be dedicated to the creation of your own opportunities. You will only think about your definite goal and how you are going to use your strength to achieve it. Every day, you will think about how you will take action to that goal. Every day.

It helped me first to identify the changes I needed to make in my life and, more importantly, it made me laser focus on my goals. I became more effective by stopping all distractions. That is what you are really looking for with this exercise, that laser focus that make the difference. From the day I discovered my core talents and skills, I set my goal to found my own company and my daily focus is on living my purpose and achieving this goal. Nothing else.

Through continuous self-reflection, we identify our values, we discover what is truly important to us, we become consciously aware of them so we can reorganise our priorities and daily life around them. That is when change really begins to happen.

For example, I realised I value time much more than money. This was critical because it made me reconsider my goals in life, my priorities and it really made me completely reorganise the way I was living. You could possibly imagine the huge impact it all had in my own leadership style. I was becoming more confident. I realised that what I liked or enjoyed the most at work was talking in public to a large audience; even though I felt nervous about it, I became aware of my talent for it so it allowed me to focus more on this particular talent development than any other area. It also guided me when choosing the sort of companies I was going to create. I tried to organise most of my life around this talent really. I feel more comfortable with this rather than using other sets of skills that I had but that I never felt good with. This is the single action that helps you to regain your hidden powers.

ARE YOU WORTHY?

"Make sure you don't start seeing yourself
through the eyes of those who don't value you.
Know your worth even if they don't."

-Thema Davis

During my first task as a graduate manager, a more senior manager unfortunately made a comment insinuating that due to my personality I would be an average manager at best. Given I had a relatively strong character, I initially overcame the situation. Considering it was my first working experience in life, it had a tremendous impact on me. I felt devastated and carried that impression with me for many years. Every time I was disappointed in anything, I would bring his words back. I allowed them to define me for so long. However, in 2012, when I hit bottom and reached my turning point, I realised that experience was not all of me. I reflected on it and began learning more about myself, then I realised that all I needed was to ensure I fully knew myself, to appreciate who I truly was and value it. The true first lesson for you in self-knowledge is to learn what makes you unique and accept that you are worthy. Through self-discovery, you will soon know who you truly are and your real value. When it happens, you won't need validation from anyone else.

Understanding and self-acceptance must be the foundation of every person to feel worthy of others' acceptance, not just knowing at a mental level, you must "feel" that you are of value. In case you have not realised, the source of all the pain and suffering we experience in any aspect of our life, including our professional life and our role as leaders, is self-acceptance; For us as individuals, one of the basic needs is to be accepted (feel worthy of others'

59

acceptance), to feel that we exist and that we are of value but for this to happen, we first need to accept ourselves. This feeling is also essential to maintain a peaceful state of mind. When we accept ourselves, we do not need others' approval.

In order to achieve this, you need to develop awareness and then believe in your own value. You need time to reflect on it, you need to go back in time and reflect on your thoughts, your feelings, emotions and the perception you have created about yourself in order to realise your own worth.

The more you develop it, the more confidence you will feel about your opinions and your own decisions. This is a long process and we need a lot of patience and courage but your motivator is to know that the clearer you are about who you are, the more you will value yourself, and this is the basis for authenticity and success.

Self-identity is the perception that we have about ourselves. Sometimes this perception is limited due to a lack of self-awareness. We tend to identify with some elements including our professional role or career, marital status and one or two personality traits. We never bother to know more about ourselves than those couple of points. This limitation was affecting me and is affecting most people in the world. I would probably call this a very poor self-identity. The perception I had about myself was tied to my occupation and a couple of traits that I thought fully represented me. The problem is that when I had no job or when I didn't like what I was doing, I struggled to find my self-identity. As a result, the perception I had about myself was poor and this is who I believed I was! Would I value myself in this condition? No. Would anyone else value me? Probably not.

When I tried to change it, I noticed that many personal development books and people in the industry recommended taking an inventory of myself and writing it down. At the beginning, I took an inventory of my character qualities, evaluated them and created resolutions to improve each of them and guess what...I never did anything about it. The reason is that for me, it was again about changing my habits without being fully convinced. This is of course a mental exercise, which requires persistence, patience and mental effort to improve and I still had no power to control my will at that moment. However, the good thing I learned from this exercise, and why it is worthy to do, is that you identify your qualities and keep them on top of your mind at all times, so it becomes a motivator to improve.

When you are totally convinced of how important it is for your development then go ahead and do it. It took me more than two years to fully understand why it was so important. But it doesn't matter how much I say, you might not move a finger until you are fully convinced that there is no other way but to go through this exercise.

So what can we do in the meantime? Well, what we must do is to apply this exercise to real life! It is all about observation, attention and concentration on our thoughts, our words, our actions and us. You, like me and anyone else, possess a great number of characteristics, roles and physical attributes, so ensure you know them very well and consciously pick or select the ones from which you create your self-identity. This is what truly represents you and the perception you have about yourself will improve immediately. The game of life will start changing for you.

THE DOMINO EFFECT

"I have learned a lot from thinking of myself as hopeless, from seeing the ego, not as something to develop and grasp at, but as something to understand and know. And from that understanding a sense of self-respect has come about."

-Ven. Ajahn Sumedho

Sort out your own perception (your self-identity) and you start changing the game of life. When you perceive yourself differently, you will start thinking, talking and acting differently. You will notice this and so will others. Here is when the domino effect starts; as your perception of yourself begins to change so does your self-image, which then influences your self-esteem. Your self-esteem contributes to your self-confidence and your self-confidence has a strong impact on your character. This is not a miracle and doesn't just happen. It is the result of hard work training your mind, which is what part two of this book is dedicated to.

When I began to see myself differently and I started to think differently about myself, I learned that the image I held about myself was strongly and emotionally tied to what I imagined others were seeing in me. Obviously, I was imagining negatively. I was judging myself and the judgement was mostly against myself. To realise this was shocking but it was a real eye-opener. Million of thoughts flooded my mind. What a new discovery! For the first time, I was truly realising that all the suffering during past experience, situations and conditions I was living with were somehow linked to the poor image I had about myself and my lack of clear self-identity. I say this because I realised my low self-esteem was the result of all this. What a new revelation! With the low opinion I had about my value to the world and to others, how could I ever become a confident leader? I mean, how can anyone become fully confident at a personal and professional level if he or she has a poor perception about themselves based on a lack of self-knowledge?

I hope I have made it very clear to you that self-confidence is built on self-esteem, which is the result of self-image and self-image is improved by self-identity and self-knowledge and do you remember what the starting point of self-knowledge is? If not, go back and read the beginning of this chapter again...

Now, self-confidence is not only one of the most important traits or qualities of a leader, but it is the key element of a strong character. This is the first point I wanted to reach! Because from here I could say a lot but I prefer to go back to the beginning of this book and briefly argue that perhaps one of the most important reasons why leaders and people like us in general have a poor performance is because we lack a strong character.

As a society, we forgot about this. In modern times, we value are more concerned with personality rather than character. Our culture and modern literature, including the most popular and influential books such as Dale Carnegie's "How To Win Friends And Influence People", emphasised the concept of personality and forget the value of "character".

Character is the basis for the degree of success of any man and it is one of the most recognised and popular traits of authentic and successful people. Just listen to any of the great leaders, scientists, artists or businessmen and you will immediately recognise a great character in them.

Every time we learn more about our true self, we are gaining emotional intelligence, learning to understand others and strengthening our character. These three are terrific qualities, particularly for a leader or manager; however, the strengthening of character is the most important by far. A strong character is indispensable for personal success in every area. Therefore, the most important outcome of self-knowledge must be to strengthen and develop a successful, winning character. This is possible because it is within our control. We do not need to change others, we do not need to fight external circumstances, we only need to focus on ourselves. Start with self-awareness and aim to strengthen your character. Now you know how to do it. This is the first element of how to be successful while being authentic. The other two will be explained in steps two and three, but these two are dependent upon character.

William Ganson in his book "Success in Business" recognised character as one of the three essential factors for success in anything but particularly in business and there's no need to mention the importance of being truly authentic. With this aim in mind, you can either become a great leader with a strong character or an abusive leader with an evil character. The former will build a joyful environment for others, the latter will create a toxic organisation.

I learned most of my knowledge about character and how to strengthen it from that book. The building up and strengthening of character involves not only the improvement of its qualities but the management of them. The management of these qualities involve the study of your mental attitude, one of the most important phases of character research, and this requires the understanding and application of two forces: desire and will. These forces are there to develop a success-winning character. These two forces are the soul of this personal growth journey. I wrote step two and three to pass you the knowledge of how to train to control desire and will. Nevertheless, I can tell you now that it is by winning small battles day by day that you begin strengthening these forces and you will be developing a success-winning character.

I would like to close this chapter by mentioning that this whole self-discovery journey, from self-awareness to self-knowledge to strengthening of character, requires thought and those thoughts would be better if the senses necessary to perceive them are used. Among the senses, the eyes and ears are the most important for observation and attention. To develop them, we have to train them. Observe and listen rather than see and hear!. If we observe, attend and concentrate, we are extracting a meaning out of something.

It requires observation, attention and concentration to understand something deeply and to be able to create something better out of it (whatever it is). Do not forget we are consciously looking for awareness of our thoughts, emotions, feelings, etc. This is all you have to do for now. Every day. If you forget one day, it doesn't matter, just do it every time you remember it.

However, do not forget you are now training your brain, and as any other muscle, it is all about repetition and practice. We are collecting information about ourselves. With time, we will understand ourselves and then we will develop the capacity for judging ourselves. This is vital to learn and be able to take responsibility. Remember, great leaders know when to take responsibility and blame themselves. Why do we want to blame ourselves? Simple, you find room for improvement, room to grow, to develop your full potential. If we keep blaming others, we will never change, we will never grow...we will disappear.

The method of self-awareness for everyday practise is constant effort to avoid slipshod thinking and to observe keenly. Continue doing this process, day by day, until it becomes a habit so you do not require mental effort anymore. You will realise first that you have developed an increased devotion to study yourself and secondly, perhaps by default, you have developed self-discipline and unconquerable determination to master your thoughts, words and actions. Now you are in the process of building a real foundation to critical thinking, complex problem solving, judgement and decision-making. That is distilled knowledge, and that is wisdom. Be consciously aware of it and know you are valuable, you are worthy!

When you are aware of who you are and your value, you have practically beaten one of the most powerfully limiting emotions of any man: the fear of rejection. This will set you free as you are no longer defined by what others think or what you might think about yourself.

You have also created a positive attitude about yourself. This positive attitude will influence and improve your attitude about others because the more you learn about yourself, the more you understand what happens to other people. Understanding others at this core level is very powerful. It gives you an increased ability to influence people as your level of consciousness is higher than most. This is key for success in life and particularly in business. So go ahead and begin right now to become more aware of yourself. Stop reading and think how you are feeling right now and identify why you are feeling like that. Go to the source, to the bottom of that feeling, explore it and learn from it. Remember: self-awareness and then self-knowledge and that character is the vital foundation for authenticity.

Chapter 3.

DECIDE WHO YOU WANT TO BE

"I think it is possible for ordinary people to choose to be extraordinary."

-Elon Musk.

THE MOTIVATION FORCE

*"Your purpose in life is to find your purpose
and give your whole heart and soul to it."*

– Buddha

Know what you want! Isn't it sad that we have been living for many years and we are still not confident answering this question? Certainly it is sad, but equally sad is that we are not clear what our purpose in life is. Our vision? Our purpose? What difference does it make? And is it really important? Here I will answer it in a simple and clear way, starting with purpose.

Purpose is the difference between joy and whatever the opposite of it is. Do you understand that? Do you realise the magnitude of that sentence? I am not telling you to understand any management technique, or any leadership theory or tool set, no! I am telling you about the key to truly have a joyful life.

Really, there is no need to judge, analyse or debate this statement. Simply accept it, convince yourself about its truth, believe it and start living it.

Your purpose is the original reason why you came to this world, or simply, what you can do for *someone else*. What is the effort you make for others? Having a definite purpose in your life brings you an instant, continuous and permanent state of happiness and annihilates suffering. This is obviously vital for a great life and is essential for great leadership. I'll explain why.

Happiness can be only received when it's given, thus, when you have an unchanging purpose to do something for others, a faithful intention to give and to serve others so they can be and enjoy happiness, it produces a motivational energy because it connects with the heart as well as the head when you realise your true impact on other people's lives. That's purpose.

Every human being, including our leaders, naturally and permanently look for happiness, particularly their own happiness; you and me, as any other human being, naturally want to be happy ourselves before even thinking about someone else's happiness. However, when serving others becomes the essential belief in our new mindset, we stop that horrible feeling of constantly chasing happiness and we start living joyfully day by day. This is when you gladly answer "I am living my purpose" while you see many other people suffering as they do not seem to find happiness in what they do.

A clear life purpose is another essential quality that most of our leaders lack. Unfortunately, traditional leadership education doesn't seem to understand its vital importance for someone who is training to lead and support a group of people. If a person's purpose is to give happiness and serve others, we can say that this person is a natural leader and will surely have followers.

Having a definite purpose or being conscious of your purpose in life is one of the most important values you can ever gain.

It will give you mental and spiritual power. It fills your mind with determination and converts it into an amazing source of energy. These two benefits alone will make you a completely different person. They are the source of positive thinking, a great attitude, new positive habits and behaviours and the most important benefit is the extraordinary feeling of gratitude.

After experiencing the lowest point in my life, when I felt miserable at work, living a meaningless life and suffering the pain of this feeling and learning the lessons the hard way, I started making changes and I saw amazing improvements. I noticed that what might seem impossible at that time was absolutely possible for me and if I was able to raise myself from that undesirable life situation, I was convinced it was absolutely possible for anyone else to do it too.

The first thing I thought was that I didn't want my children or any other member of my family to ever be in that situation of living life in stress, depression, frustration or even tiredness states as so painful and I did not want anyone to live or remain living like that. That was my very truthful feeling of compassion for others. As I tuned into it, I started to realise that many people were suffering by living a meaningless life. I realised that some of them were prisoners of their jobs, prisoners of their bosses, prisoners of their time and their money.

From that moment, there was only one thing in this world that I was determinate to achieve: to use my creative mind and willingness to express ideas to inspire others to find themselves and then coach them to grow to higher levels and live more profound lives so we all can enjoy a better world. I thought the best way to do it would be to help develop authentic and successful leaders who can in turn help the rest of humanity to grow, have a better life and change our world.

As soon as I felt I had found a definite reason for my life, I committed to it, I focused on it, I filled my thoughts with it, I talked to myself about it and begin to imagine it. I focussed all my energy, all my will power and all my effort, everything, to back that definite purpose.

I left everything behind me and staked my entire future on developing the abilities I needed to live my definite purpose. This is to say, I committed to a life-long self-development as I was fully convinced this was the only path. Every day I just want to be better, I feel I need to be better so I can fulfil my purpose. Living my purpose is now a continuously evolving journey that has no final destination. I can't stop this feeling and I do not feel I will ever give up. This is the sort of emotion or feeling or desire that needs to be created to live a fulfilling and successful life.

This was a dramatic change in my life and since that moment, everything I do, I do it with this purpose in mind. I realised then that it is about living your purpose in what you do every moment and for this, you only have to change your mind set.

I shifted my focus from myself to something higher than me. At that point, I realised I was learning to lead myself first and I truly understood what leadership was all about (a great lesson for Authentic Leadership). My message is to work on this before you try to improve any leadership or management skills.

To discover your life purpose, you must first be convinced that this is more important than anything else at this moment. If you think that your job is important, think twice; this is more important as you will work much better when you have a clear personal purpose. If you think that your finances or social life or your relationship is more important, again think twice. At this moment, discovering your purpose is much more important as it will be your foundation for a stronger financial situation, better relationships and social life.

If you are fully convinced, then move on and focus on understanding yourself at a deeper level of your passions and your underlying motivations. This is why we looked at these first in the previous chapter. Understanding yourself means accepting the concept of you as the whole person paradigm because you need to consider your body, your mind, spirit and heart; your purpose is the purpose of all of them together. Only considering your physical will make you believe that a definite material goal is your purpose. That is one of the commonest mistakes in modern society.

Do not ask anyone else about your purpose. It is not out there. No one has the knowledge or the right to tell you what it should be. It is up to you to discover it, and again, it is inside you alone.

To truly embrace your real purpose, you must develop the ability to control your mind so you can shift the focus from yourself to others. To control the mind is to be able to calm it so it feels peaceful first. If the mind is not wandering around, if you are able to understand how your mind works, you will recognise the attachments that might affect your true purpose to serve others and you will reduce your suffering.

You need to reflect on it. The key is to give time to yourself time to think and if you reflect on it for as long as necessary, you will awaken a sort of sensation that will guide you throughout your search. At this point, I started developing an interest in meditation as a technique to calm my mind. I recommend you to read and make yourself familiar with this ancient technique that is essential for our self-development.

As you are creating your definite purpose, mindfulness and conscious self-talk are very helpful. In my mind, I saw myself asking what I really wanted, exactly what I wanted. You then begin to command your mind, requesting its support and you are consciously awakening this energy that will become the governing principle of your life. I am sorry if it sounds a bit weird but this is exactly what happens. Research some of the greatest minds of our time, listen carefully to them and you will start hearing these ideas in their conversations.

Talking to myself? This might sound a bit crazy or you might think I've lost it…well, if you are thinking that, you might well know that you have been doing that too though perhaps unconsciously, which is the actual issue. Most of your self-talk is most probably negative, so all I am asking you is to consciously change it and start talking in a more positive way to yourself.

We need (from a very young age by the way) to consciously talk to ourselves every day and ask ourselves what we will do with our lives? I knew that I had at least one talent, so my question became how I could use it to live my purpose and succeed? From there, I created the ideal of my life and I finally committed to make of myself a man of ability and character to merit it.

You will have to dedicate an exclusive time during the day, every day for the now forgotten action of thinking (pure thinking). In my mind, what I tried to do was to see myself asking "what do I want, exactly what do I really want the most in my life". Do not get discouraged if you do not see or feel any progress or change. Just keep doing for as long as it takes! It is the purpose of your life! Your only life! If you follow this, you will soon begin getting signs from your inner-self, which is your true self.

Listen to yourself: it is you inside you telling you and pushing you to be better or nobler or higher. This is life, this is the purpose of life. A good way to recognise it is to reflect back on your past. Do a conscious examination of all the main events and actions in your past, which have had a great impact on your life. Meditate on it, and if you need, write it down or draw something that represents them. Search carefully, it is there, and if you take this exercise seriously, you will see it jump in front of your eyes. You should consider this as one of the most important moments of your life.

Naturally, you will realise that your purpose is related to those particular actions that you simply love doing. It must be like that because the universe knows that you will need to develop a burning desire to achieve it, and the only way you will have this immense desire is by having a real passion for it. Put simply, you love it!.

Having created your purpose, you must mentally create a road map to its attainment. This is your pathway, never look right, never look left, look straight ahead.

You should align your personal vision, your goals and everything else with your life purpose.

SEEING BEYOND THE OBVIOUS

"Your vision is the promise of what you shall one day be.
Your ideal is the prophecy of what you shall at last unveil."

-James Allen

To move to a higher level, we must have a clear and definite purpose, but we must also see what is worthy of achieving while in life.

When I was clear about my purpose, or the main reason why I am in this planet, I started thinking about finding my own personal vision or definite goal, that activity I would love doing that also allowed me to live my purpose every day. I asked myself, what is this goal that would enable me to develop to my fullest potential and enjoy living my life purpose? For me, finding an answer to this question was the logical step to follow.

From purpose, now we are moving to find our own personal vision or definite goal. I truly believe this is the order, as creating a definite goal or aim without considering your highest purpose is to fall in the physical world, aiming for the material but never reaching the internal peace and the feeling of living a significant life.

In relation to creating a definite goal or vision to aim for in our life, the key lesson I learned is that before deciding what to pursue, it is worthy to know what is wisest to desire. In order to do so, we first have to develop the ability to identify the really good and great things to aspire to while in life. Without this ability, you will end up like most people, wishing for the big house, the expensive sports car or other material things.

The problem with these sorts of goals is that they will limit your potential immediately and will set you up for much less than you can achieve. This is what condemns all of us to an average life. These material things are good, don't get me wrong, having them is nice, I would never discourage you from aiming to have them too. But they can be short-term goals, and having things should never be your definite goal.

The same situation happens if your definite aim is based on doing something. To travel the world, for example, is a great goal, but should not be your definite vision. It will limit your potential as well; even though aiming to have an experience or aspiring to do something extraordinary will contribute more towards your personal development than just possessing something material, it is still not the wisest decision for something to aim towards.

What I strongly suggest you to do when trying to choose your definite goal in life is to focus your attention more on the "being" rather than the "having" or "doing". Life is about becoming more, not about doing more or having more. The key element here is to focus purely and only on who you want to become. Whoever is that person you intend to be, aim for it, aim for wisdom, for supreme self-control, aim to become a person of honour; develop the abilities required to become the person you intend to be and you will be able to do and have everything else you wish; the expensive sports car, the travels and all the other things will also come to you, should you wish so.

To be able to know what the wisest goal for you to pursue is and find who you want to become, we said you will need an "ability" to learn and to know that is higher than normal.

To develop this ability, we need to make an effort to think. You will forego the shallow pleasures of the moment and with so many distractions and so much to do, I can tell you it is not easy but if you are willing to make that effort, an increased ability will come to your assistance. By following this, you will succeed in life in a legitimate way. I do not really know how I would be able to explain this if not through my own experience.

First, with an open mind, I received an idea, I reflected on it and looked at it from different perspectives. I read much more about this until I accumulated enough information to be convinced and believed it.

From there, I included this idea of demanding a higher ability in my daily meditation. As I was anxious, I found it disconcerting at first; some people told me I should not force it but patiently wait for it, while at the same time others advised me not to ask for it but demand it! I tried both options, calmed meditation and focused thinking sessions. I believe this combination works very well for me. The time came when I finally found myself totally immersed in my vision and, more importantly, with the spirit, the purpose and a strong desire to make it real. I felt deeply grounded and grateful because my definite vision was clear and stimulating. I guess mixing the two techniques was good for me. Not so long ago, I was reading about these sorts of techniques from a Harvard college library's forgotten book and I also heard many successful people refer to it as well.

Looking back, and in more detail, I notice that the ability came when I first made the decision to dedicate time to think without regrets and when I cleared my mind of all the usual thoughts that were distractors. From that moment on, all I did was to be focused on who I wanted to become; my mind became clearer and I started seeing possibilities for me that perhaps were always there but I simply could not see before because my mind was always distracted with something else.

Be aware that this is not a matter of thinking for 5 or 10 minutes about it then jumping into the "truly" important things you need to do. I am talking about a mental exercise that should take priority over any other matter around you, including your job. It has to become a priority for you. If you are a manager, I am sure you know what to do when there is an important and urgent task, don't you? Succeeding in this exercise is the first thing that will make you believe you truly have a power you were not aware of and were not benefiting from.

I used my mind to create the person I intended to be. I "dreamed big" and then I imagined myself developed to my fullest potential! I had nothing to lose. I put together everything I had learned about myself, my strengths and skills for public speaking, my purpose to help others with their personal growth, my interest in leadership, my passion for learning about the mind and its faculties, my family and my own personal development, my strongest values, my character and even my passion for travelling... I brought it all together to create that vision of myself that I called my definite goal. I used my imagination to visualise it, to have it clear in my mind and finally I fixed all my attention on what this goal promised me for my future. This I did while fully convinced and with a strong belief that this was the path I wanted to follow and I made the decision to walk this path for the rest of my life. Since that day, all distractions became irrelevant for me.

After doing all this, it won't be strange for you when people start recognising you as highly focused, ambitious and highly determined person, who has a clear high purpose, virtue and vision.

You gain more than a skill set setting these goals or targets; these qualities are the result of having an uncontrollable desire and determination to achieve your definite goal when living your purpose.

With this in mind, your result is a definite goal that will take you as an individual and as a leader to a higher level, a Creative level.

This is all good but unfortunately, we do not act on it. Most books and training teach us goal setting in a hundred different ways, still we find difficult to change our behaviour to actually set our goal and act on it. We all have more or less the same abilities, however, some become successful than others. Few will take action on it, while others will continue living their lives in the same way. The difference is simple: Believing it.

There are some people who believe, but still do not act on it. This is why I focus the next two parts of this book on gaining the knowledge for how to desire and attain that power that will motivate you to act. Make your mind deal with yourself in a different way. Only compare yourself against your goals. You will realise that this is all a personal matter. Commit to your self-development. This is the secret of EFFICIENCY.

What sort of power or ability are we really talking about here? I will use an example that is similar to what W. Ganson uses when referring to measuring someone's financial success. According to him, financial success is measured not by the amount of dollars but by financial influence. If a man wants to earn £10k a month, his ambition must be to earn this, however, more important, his desire should be for the ability to merit this £10K a month. We must merit that amount before we can actually get it. Here is when many of us fail to work for the £10K ability. This is about changing the focus from the external ambition (whatever it is) to our internal abilities and personal development. This concept is extremely important for success as we now know that our goals depend entirely on us. So, you want to double or triple your salary? Great ambition! Then your desire should be for the ability to merit that increase. Focus on developing that ability; you must become the person who can earn triple your current salary. This must be your first step.

To create my own personal vision, I first had to believe that there was something great in the future for me. I looked up my newly discovered purpose and imagine myself fully developed in relation to it and to every area of my life. I desired that by following my purpose I would become recognised worldwide for my ideas and my talks. I dreamed big and saw myself as a world-leading speaker and coach and that all my knowledge was shared globally through my bestseller books. That was my vision only a couple of years ago, in 2012, to be precise.

So why did I take action immediately? The most important point here was to believe that this was all possible for me. First, I discovered that it was so much easier for me to believe it was possible to achieve my vision because I began with my strengths in mind. My definite goal was created and based on my own strengths. I knew I was good at speaking and sharing ideas, so I did not have to fight against many negative beliefs. I was simply clear I had the capabilities to do it.

The second point I found was the motivation I received to do it and take action immediately since I knew I would enjoy each and every bit of my journey. I knew that would be something I would love to wake up every day and do for the rest of my life. And finally, I believed I could better develop myself to become that person I wanted to be and I only had to focus on developing the ability to become that person. This helped me to start working towards that vision and I was amazed how I started achieving success from day one. When I accepted and believed my vision, I became totally indifferent to potential failure.

Even though I was immediately gaining success, this success was at a mental level at that moment and stayed there for quite a while. Physical and financial rewards tend to be so slow at first and that might discourage you. Realise that is the test for your desire and will and that is why we must persist in increasing our power. Here is when most people fail and give up. I assure you that the results are there, day by day and it will be seen particularly in your mind. Your aren't gaining physical rewards but remember that is not our aim yet, what we are aiming is for is the ability to deserve your vision, and in that sense we are gaining a lot since our self-confidence and character are growing stronger with this greater ambition, keener desire and a stronger will. Here you are developing that very famous "CAN DO" attitude from the real origin and in the right way.

When you are clear about your definite goal, put all your energy, all your willpower, all your effort and everything else into that goal. Do not have another option or plan "B" different to your goal. It is about developing the abilities necessary to get what you truly want. From that moment, you will have to work on getting that power to become so determined to have it that you convince yourself that you will have it. Once again, this is only possible through the processes explained in part 2 and 3 of this book.

It is now your responsibility to look after this new condition. You are now getting close to being in pure harmony with the universe. You are closer to the creation force.

Your purpose and your definite aim will guide you and will help you to remove all the extras in your life. More importantly, your decision-making process will be so simple and so acquired that people will start noticing your wisdom without much propaganda.

Now you know exactly the person you would like to become.

Thus, when making a decision, your mind will naturally make a quick consultation and ask itself, would this decision take me closer or further from my definite goal? This makes your decision process very straightforward and the side-effect of this is nothing less than an increase in self-confidence. Purpose is good, shared purpose is better. When you know your purpose, you will turn your company upside down to follow it. You are immediately building a truly authentic organisation that will engage customers and employees in a more compassionate way.

As a result of your purpose and your growing desire for its achievement, you will soon feel the need to organise your life around it. You know you will need resources and skills to achieve it so it is crucial to create a clear plan of how you are going to achieve it.

Here is when the game, "your game", really takes off. You must first be clear and very specific about your purpose, so you will spend more time contemplating it; you also want to enjoy the journey to its attainment, so your plan will be to design the lifestyle you would be happy to live. The concept we are talking about at this point is "Your Life Plan".

THE ORACLE - LIFE PLANNING

"The sooner you start planning your life,
the sooner you will live the life you dream of."

-Hans Glint.

It was the 15th of February 2013 when I found myself sitting in one of the reading rooms of the British Library trying to find out what exactly I wanted to achieve in life, who I wanted to become and how I would organise my life. I spend two full days in the library sitting exactly in the same place just thinking and reflecting on it.

I chose to start by looking at myself as the whole-person paradigm. I personally used the four dimensions: body, soul, heart and mind as the base to plan the life I wanted to live my purpose. Development of these three dimensions was my definite goal. From each of these dimensions I selected the areas or priorities in my life.

As a result, my six priority areas were family, career, health, finance, social and spiritual life. I considered which were the most important in my life and I ranked them.

For each of them I created three sorts of goals, one for what I wanted to be, then what I wanted to do and then what I wanted to have. I focused on understanding first, who I wanted to be or become in relation to that particular area then I looked at what I needed to do to achieve it and finally what I wanted to have when I achieved it. This is a second great stage as you are shifting your aim and goals from the "having" or "doing" culture to the "being". This is fundamental for an authentic leader as you shift what you value from getting to actually experiencing or, even better, living.

Imagination and dream big are the concepts I must highlight during this particular part of the process. I couldn't agree more with Napoleon Hill, that we hardly use our imagination, at least not in the correct way. We simply do not understand the immense power of this faculty yet. I will talk a bit more in detail in the second part of this book but in the meantime I can tell you that it was during this exercise that I made the correct use of my imaginative faculty for the first time.

At this point, I would like to stop my story and grab your attention to the key points here. When we are ready to create our own future and commit the rest of our life to the achievement of these definite plans, there are two main recommendations for you to do. First, be wise when deciding what you desire in your life so you do not focus all your potential on something that is not worthy and second, dream big, really big. To achieve these two aspects, you need a very smart use of your imagination.

Back to my story. That exercise was purely a thinking, reflecting and even meditating exercise. Every line I wrote was carefully considered in my context and was evaluated before being included.

I made sure these decisions were in line with my values, my beliefs, my capabilities, my dreams and also that they would contribute to the improvement of others, including, of course, my family's life.

I essentially looked at what I wanted to achieve when I was close to my final days. I wrote in detail the sort of actions and activities I would love to do and that would take me to my definite goal and I set reasonable deadlines for each and every single item in my list. It took me almost two full days to finish it. By the second day, I was completely devoted to become the person I really wanted to be. Naturally, it can take longer for some or shorter for others. It is an individual process and you are the one to decide how much time you need for it.

When I wrote it, I look at it for a while and tried to make sure it was very clear for me. I meditated, I slept on it, I reflected about it again and I finally committed to its achievement. I visualized all my goals together again and I named it "my life purpose".

That simple action of "automatic writing" has been one the most important documents I have created in my life. This was the first exercise that helped me to bring my dream into reality.

It was a great feeling seeing the dreams and ideas in my mind, which ended up as a very detailed mind map. It was the best investment I have ever done in myself. It was probably the first time I dedicated time to thinking purely about myself. Every second, minute and hour I spent contemplating, imagining and visualizing it was worthy, as I felt so clear, so focused and so motivated to become the person I am meant to be. I almost instantly developed that strong burning desire to attain my definite goal.

After drawing my life plan on a piece of paper, I wanted to make sure it would always remain close to me, so I thought it would be a good idea to have it on my mobile phone. I downloaded a mind map app and used it to draw my life plan, made it digital and saved it on my phone so I could carry it with me to use as my most important stimulator or motivator to take daily actions. Since that day, every morning and every night, I look at my sacred map. Just to see and read it fills me with a vital power that includes faith, will, decision, optimism, courage and the power of intention. Feeling this vital power is something magical.

One thing I now know is that we often have this strong feeling, but the difference is that this time I created it consciously and more important, I was perfectly aware of it. I realised I was slowly discovering my inner wisdom, that wisdom that exists in every one of us, that wisdom I expect you to discover if you reflect on this reading.

I have carried this with me since 2012 and I have been able to focus all my daily activities to the achievement of those goals. I promised myself that I would not do anything other than action what I have written in there and anything else that would contribute to their achievement.

From that moment, I stopped doing any other activity that was not linked to it. For instance, it was the first time in my life that in spite of not having a job, and I really needed one, I consciously, happily and with clear determination rejected a good job offer. I knew that job would not take me to my definite goals and I knew in my heart that it would be wrong for me, for my life and for the universe to use my talents and capabilities and apply them to something I would not love doing and I would not be able to give my 100%.

These sort of decisions that were previously difficult for me, and that I would have made wrongly most of the time, became so easy, quick and rewarding. For the first time, I did not have doubts over my decisions being good or bad, I simply knew it was the right decision for me and my family. In fact I can say that the decisions, the key decisions in my life, were taken that day I decided to create my life plan and took the needed time to do it and involved not just the things I wanted to have in life, but what I wanted to do and, more importantly, who I wanted to be.

Every day in the morning and in the afternoon, I look at my mind map and know in advance that I will make all the right decisions as long as they are in line with my life plan. I know I will have a great day as I will be doing all the activities I dreamed of and wanted to do. And I know that I am building my future and I am getting close to my goals every day. So life stopped happening TO me and began happening FOR me!.

Since that day, every day as soon as I wake up and every evening just before I go to bed, I consciously look at it in order to keep my mind focused at all times. This simple exercise became my daily self-motivation, my permanent source of inspiration, and the torch that guides me and keeps away any distraction so I stay on my path.

By modelling this process, you can have a clear and focused vision of your chief aim which is essential for your personal growth. It is your compass that will keep you heading in the right direction at all times. This is the first step and the first key element of our new mindset. It will positively influence your mental attitude, but it does not guarantee us the attainment and the enjoyment of success. For this, we also need the other two steps and/or vital components that will influence our mental attitude: knowledge and energy.

Thus, these three elements together are the key to secure success of any kind. Moreover, the clarity of the vision (knowledge) and the strength of that energy or desire could easily be the difference between success and failure. In fact, the reality is that success and failure both depend on our mental attitude.

I say it again, "success and failure both depend on our mental attitude". This is an impressive statement that gives great importance to our mental attitude. I took it as advice and focused all my energy on understanding it, not knowing that this was the key element that makes our vision into something real, the reality of success, as written several years ago by Neville Goddard. How it happens and how it works is what I am going to explain in the next chapter (Step two of our process).

For free resources including my personal life-planning template please contact me or register at www.theclearmindedleader.com

END OF PART ONE.

PART 2

BUILD A CLEAR MIND

STEP 2. ACQUIRE THE KNOWLEDGE

(KNOW THE LAWS AND CONDITIONS)

Ch. 4. This second step explains the process to develop mental strength through understanding the subconscious mind and the way it works. It describes a self-training method to build a well-guarded mind that can be vigilant by watchfulness. It explains how simple actions can help maintain a peaceful state of mind that can endure abuse in peace.

Ch. 5. It tells about the training of the mind to develop a positive thinking and positive attitude that build mental habits and the ability to speak and act with a pure mind.

Chapter 4.

THE TRAINING OF YOUR MIND

"My greatest challenge has been to change the mindset of people. Mindsets play strange tricks on us. We see things the way our minds have instructed our eyes to see".

-Muhammad Yunus

BEGINNING RIGHT

*"There is only one thing that makes a dream
impossible to achieve: the fear of failure."*

– Paulo Coelho

For this part of the book, I am first taking the role of a researcher and then that of a teacher to explain what I learned from my research. I am not a psychologist or philosopher or neuroscientist or any related profession. I have been trained in business and I am a passionate reader and a teacher who loves to explain concepts. Anything I have written in these following chapters are my thoughts, ideas and understanding of my own experience by applying the research work of many extraordinary scientists and psychologists of the most prestigious universities and labs in the world, cross-compared with manuscript of ancient Asian philosophy (Buddhism and Taoism) and the work of many authors from the nineteenth century. For the last four years, I have been reading about it and I simply want to share this extraordinary knowledge with anyone who, for whatever reason, simply hasn't had access to it.

If you start working on developing self-awareness as explained in step one, you will soon realise that you are much clearer about who you are and who you want to become. This is the key element for authenticity and necessary for success. You are probably committed to develop the abilities and become the person you need to be in order to achieve your definite goal; however, you and I both know that this commitment is very weak at the moment and you can easily give up and break it, just as 98% of the people who start anything new would do. The reason is that we rarely have the required desire and belief to take action, and even when we decide to take action, we soon find that we do not have the strength and mental attitude to persevere and beat all the obstacles, challenges and barriers that surely will appear in our journey, so we end by giving up on our dreams.

It seems that there are two different problems here, a lack of desire to pursue our goal and a lack of mental strength to continue in spite of all barriers. However, the source of both problems is pretty much the same: doubts, anxiety, worries and fear of failure. These negative feelings are our worst enemies. Doubts, fear, anxiety and worries must be deleted completely from your mind. They put us in a state of mind that does not allow us to grow, to develop, to change, to learn, to progress. They only exist in our mind but they are the biggest and most difficult obstacles to overcome in life's success. If you do not conquer them, you thwart yourself at every step; in fact, nothing will be possible for you if they are not eliminated.

Fear is one of the strongest human emotions and the primary obstacle for personal growth. It will attack you badly simply because it does not like change. I already told you my story, it was full of this negative emotion. Fear comes with the "classic" feeling that result from thoughts such as, who do I think I am? or I am not good enough. You cannot do it and so on and so.

Fear can be expressed through worry. In every aspect of your life, your mind should be clear, positive and confident, if we want to enjoy life fully, live our purpose and achieve our goal; but if we worry, this is impossible. You will lose clarity because worry confuses the mind; you can be positive because worry introduces doubts and you can't be fully confident because worry brings dread.

Moreover, one worry leads to another, and too many worries lead to failure. When you worry about losing your job, soon you will be worry about how you will pay the mortgage then you will worry about losing your house and so on.

On the other hand, if you are now worried about your work, just like millions of other people, reflect on it and you will see that it is not the work, or hard work you should fear; it is work accompanied by worry that produces most of the failure. Moreover, though most of our worries are small and simple, they still affect us a lot.

Therefore, we must train our mind, we must build the right mindset that will underpin that strong and positive mental attitude required first, to take action and second, to face every obstacle that appears in our journey so you do not give up when trying to become all you want to be.

Notice that I said: build the right mindset that underpins the mental attitude. The two key elements of your mental attitude are your thoughts and your feelings. Keep that in mind because this is what we want to master, our thoughts and feelings. To do so, we must work on our mindset.

By the way, when I began training my mind, there were times when I barely saw any progress and I felt discouraged so I know that might discourage you too. However, be persistent because progress is being made in your mind. It is building up in the same way you develop muscle with continuous exercise.

And finally, remember that success is not merely a destination that, once reached, we will enjoy the results but rather, it is the experience of being who we are, being authentic and becoming something greater. It is about creating a joyful journey towards our definite goal and truly living every day of our life doing what you love. Do not forget it.

THE MINDSET EFFECT

"In our own lives, having a mind-set of expecting to win increases our odds of winning. It helps us get better results. And better results help us increase our credibility and self-confidence, which leads to more positive self-expectancy, and more winning - and the upward cycle continues. It becomes a self-fulfilling prophecy."

-Stephen Covey

I was sitting on my bed talking on the phone to my sister discussing the bad results I was having in different areas of my life. I argued that for many years, I expected to build a fit and healthy body that would make me feel more confident, but as much as I wished, I never achieved good results. It was my New Year's resolution for over a decade but every time I took a little action and began working on it and saw no big improvements in short time, I lost the motivation and the interest and quickly forgot about it. Many times I signed up to different gyms or started practicing a sport or simply decided to change my habits and start jogging or walking more but after a few weeks I knew I would get bored, make excuses and I would stop doing it. Then I would blame my lack of commitment and discipline as the cause of my poor results and I would go back to my old routine. At that moment, she interrupted me and excitedly mentioned that one of her friends at university had completely transformed her life going from being the classic "looser" into becoming highly successful. Not only that, she had achieved financial independence and was better in all areas of her life. She said she looked very confident, relaxed, healthier and had a contagious sense of enthusiasm and energy. To be honest, I wasn't so interested until she said something that got my attention, she said, "It all had to do with her mindset and mental attitude". She didn't say anything else, she did not know anything else.

But that was more than enough for me to engage in daily research on the topic. After a while, I discovered she was right, it was all to do with our mindset. We all know, and it is pretty obvious for us, that our results depend on our actions and behaviour. This is the law of cause and effect. Do something and you get one result, do nothing and you get a different result. Naturally, every time we want to improve, be better, grow or simply change something, we take action, we invest time and money learning a new skill or changing a habit with the hope that it changes our results. However, most of the time these changes in actions have little or no impact on our results. Moreover, many times it is difficult or hard just to take action. We want a better house, or a better job, or a healthy body, we wish we could have it, but still we do nothing, we do not take action, we just stay the same, even if we aren't happy.

It turns out that our action and behaviour are influenced by our expectations; having high expectations or having low expectations will make us take different actions. If your expectation is to have a high leadership position in a large organisation, surely you will take different actions than if your expectation is to have a low responsibility part-time job. What is more interesting is to know that our expectations are highly influenced by our mental attitude; so having low expectations about ourselves and our future is the result of a not so positive mental attitude and guess what, our mental attitude depends on our mindset.

Therefore, our mindset is responsible for a particular state of mind and that mental attitude is pretty much originally responsible for our great or poor performance and results. Moreover, we can pretty much guarantee that the results we achieve are going to reinforce those original beliefs in our mind.

This would be all good if not for the fact that we are full of negative beliefs that are the cause of around 45,000 negative thoughts a day (according to many mind research and articles), which evolve into fear, doubt and worry, creating this typical "failure consciousness" in our mind. That is our problem.

95

From that day on, I decided to focus most of my energy and time on learning, understanding our belief system and mindset and how to take control of it so I could ensure the results I expected to have.

I started using this concept as a framework to look at every aspect and every result I had in my life and related it to my beliefs. I also looked at other people's results and I saw a pattern; it was simply the law of cause and effect and, incredibly, it all started making sense to me. With a bit of discipline, I conducted an almost daily study about what thoughts and beliefs were guiding my expectations and influencing my behaviour and actions.

For instance, during my childhood, I was always among the top 5 in the class, but never the number one. I tracked back my behaviours, actions and habits and realised that I never studied as much as I could have done, I never gave my 100%, but until now I never questioned why, simply, and I say simply, because it is now very clear for me that ...simply I never expect to be the number one. Then if I now ask myself for the first time after more than 30 years why I didn't expect to be the number one in the class, it is very easy to realise that I never believed I could do it; I never believed I was the most intelligent; I was good, but not good enough for number one. That was my state of mind that influenced my attitude.

No need to say that I applied this "mindset concept or framework" to every area of my life where I had good and bad results and it was very clear to me. I finally discover the true reasons behind my results.

I now enjoy watching the performance of teams, professionals, sportspeople and, of course, managers and leaders, and I always try to identify what beliefs are limiting or supporting them to achieve better results. The "All-Blacks", the New Zealand national rugby union team, is one of my favourite examples of this and there are plenty of books dedicated to other high performance athletes, tennis players and golfers.

I understood how my national football team went to play in the world cup, managed to go through the first stage and went immediately out after losing the following game. Our team coach had previously informed the players and the whole country that they would be kind of "heroes" if they just got through the first stage. That was the expectation, nothing else! The belief that they couldn't go further than that because they weren't good enough to basically guarantee their performance and the result obviously reinforced their original belief.

This is what happens in business, in any company and in any team; leaders and team members have already pre-established limiting beliefs which could have a positive impact on their performance but most of the time it's negative. That is why when I saw the McKinsey & Company report on leadership I mentioned in the introduction, I had the feeling that was one of the main reasons for leaders' poor performance.

A good example from a product manufacturing company I used to work for are salespeople who are sent to train in sales skills but inside they know, feel and believe they are not good at selling. Their state of mind and mental attitude are not right so they come back from the training in exactly the same condition. They do not expect big changes from training so they take little action and, of course, have the same poor results which in turn reinforce the belief that they aren't good at sales.

This is a fundamental knowledge for anyone who wants to improve in any area, but particularly for leaders and those who manage people or are responsible for results and targets. Understanding and consciously applying this concept is one of the key elements to secure success at a personal and professional level.

Not so long ago, one of the leaders of a youth project in Africa proudly told me that they had bought hundreds of copies of a great book on developing "successful habits" to give to the youth for their personal development. This is a beautiful act, however, what is most probably going to happen is that those who read the book may not even take action and the few who decided to implement it might find it very hard to create these new habits, particularly if they are in contradiction to their belief systems; not to mention those who do not believe in reading as a way of learning. Yes, developing or creating good habits is essential, but those habits won't last and will not make any difference if our expectations and mindset do not support them. The only way is to change our mindset.

Changing our mindset involves the improvement of six elements; (1) identity, (2) competences, (3) values, (4) motivation force, (5) beliefs and (6) mental strategies.

The first three elements are part of your self-knowledge and we already covered it. The fourth one (motivation force) is what we referred to as your vision. That's the reason why me needed to do this in the first part of this book. If you have followed it, you are already in the process of building a new mindset. Once again, this must be your definite vision, not a short-term goal or objective to achieve and it has to be very clear in your mind, totally related with your life purpose and should be the reason for every single goal or objective you pursue in any area of your life, including your career and professional life.

In part two of this book, we will look into the fifth element, creating a strong belief system and the sixth one, the mental strategies that support that "CAN DO attitude" and the mental states of "faith and belief". You probably have your vision by now, but you are not ready for it until you believe you can attain it. Your state of mind must be belief! Not mere hope or wish. Here once again, I need to remind you about open–mindedness which is essential for belief. A closed mind does not inspire faith, courage or belief. Essentially, what we are going to do is to learn the art of changing our minds from failure consciousness to success consciousness. The focus is on developing the mental condition that pushes us to take immediate action towards our purpose and vision. This is true power.

I knew I had to be fully convinced that I could achieve my new vision, otherwise I wouldn't do anything about it and I would be disappointed for being only a dreamer who just "wished" for things without ever taking action! That would have been devastating for me and for my family who was supporting me in this journey.

To be fully convinced, every day, I dedicated all my time and energy into create the belief and the faith that my definite vision would be attained so I could develop the force and energy to act on it and persevere.

I worked on my mental attitude, but it was hard because of the fear of failing miserably. I used all the techniques I could find to fight my fears and obsessive negative thinking. To be honest, it is not easy to fight your thoughts in your own mind. I know it might sound strange, but to fight my thoughts, I first allowed myself to look for peace and calm outside my mind. I started meditating. In meditation, you go beyond the mind. I read once: *"your only chance of finding peace is to transcend the mind"* and the only possible way I know is through meditation.

A few weeks after doing this inner work, I had enough self-belief, courage and the required energy to take my very first little step. I made a call to an almost unknown person, who a few weeks later, would become not only my business partner but my perfect platform to entry the African market with my own business.

My self-belief and the faith that I could become the person I really wanted to be was vital for me to take action, and strongly increased my expectation about the result. This higher expectation of building a multinational training organisation drove greater actions from my side and a completely different behaviour. I felt more confident, communicated more effectively, made better decisions and it naturally transformed into better results.

My new business partner believed in me, and, to say it in a more spiritual way (not religious way though), he had faith in me and was willing to collaborate. That was a huge win for my newly founded business but more important, it increased my self-confidence more. This is the cycle and this cycle is progressive, the more you believe you can achieve your goal or the expected result, the higher your expectation, the stronger your actions and the better the results. It's that simple. This is the true origin of self-motivation and the real energy behind it. And it only comes from within.

When you master this principle, you will never run out of energy to work on the achievement of your goal. Other matters will never distract you and you will be far more effective in terms of your results. Any external attempt to get motivated will not last for long. Thus, motivational talks, books, videos are only short "pick me up" solutions that won't keep leaders and teams focused on their goals in the long run.

But how can we achieve this? And not only for us but for each member of our team or our family? First, let's focus on ourselves as only when we master ourselves will we be able to help or support our team. Otherwise, it is the blind leading the blind.

THOUGHTS

"The control of your mind is most important,
and it will be worth your while.
You must think deeply. Clear your mind of all bad,
unwanted thoughts"

-William O'Brien

A man must control his thoughts before he is in a position to control affairs and to adopt serious responsibilities. In other words, little or no ability to control your thoughts is an indication of a lack of self-control, which is a key element of character and essential for success.

The statement "You live in a world with an average of 80% negative thoughts" reinforces the previous message. This statement was shocking to me and grew my interest in the topic. Clearly I was part of it, however, the most incredible news for me was in the second line of this statement when I read: "*Right at this moment you can abandon it and make it a better world for you by changing to a state of mind of faith and believe.*"

It is not an exaggeration to say that this statement brought back the hope I had lost after so many disappointments in a meaningless career and professional life. I decided to believe in it completely. No questions, no judgement, I just accepted. It is one of my best decisions ever. For me, it was never about whether it was true or not, it was simply me taking it as a principle of life.

To abandon all my negative thoughts and change my state of mind or mental attitude became my biggest concern. I wanted to fix my mind on the development of my plan and the strengthening of my resolution and self-reliance, but I knew that not fighting those negative emotions would delay my own success.

To develop the true feeling of belief and faith that you will achieve your goal, you must take action and you need to take it one little step at the time to ensure that this little action is successful. I built this mental attitude day by day. In this way, you are creating evidence of your ability and this is proof to our own mind that you have the capacity and the ability. Every little successful action builds up and creates a belief from there and this belief convinces your mind.

My first action was to make the effort to be aware of my thoughts as much as I could during the day and do whatever was possible to change them if they were negative. The key for this is to focus our attention on our thoughts; a continuous effort in right thinking is our task in this developmental stage.

In the beginning, I constantly forgot about it then when I was suddenly aware of my thoughts, I realised that I had been entertaining negative thoughts for a while. I used to feel angry about it and tried to be more alert again but it was nearly impossible as I got easily distracted and again the negative thoughts were there affecting the way I was feeling. I realised every new situation was an effect so I kept linking it with the thought that caused it.

When training the mind, watch out for your thoughts consciously, study and analyse them constantly. Never surrender, learn from them, control them and make the right choice of thoughts then master their application in the right way. This you can do. It all occurs within ourselves. Do it all the time, be patient and persistent. You are obtaining knowledge about yourself, which is understanding, knowledge and energy. Here, we are realising and slowly understanding the power of our thoughts.

My second action after thoughts-awareness became a bit easier for me was much more interesting and powerful. With the help of my wife, I went further into identifying those low-energy thoughts such as criticism, comparison or judgemental thoughts. Every time me or my wife found each other making a negative comment about someone else, we immediately reacted and pointed out that the comment was sourced from a negative thought. I realised how indulgent I was in this sort of self-destructive way of thinking. Together we helped each other to lift our thoughts above that slavish animal indulgence. This is very important in order to think clearly, righteousness and speak with a pure mind.

What I noticed was that we found ourselves concentrating most of our thoughts on the search for knowledge or for the beautiful truth in life and nature. We developed the intention to cultivate a vigilant watchfulness and aimed to entertain as much noble thoughts in our daily life as possible as the benefits were clearly appreciated in our increasingly positive mental attitude and self-harmony. This is something that is highly appreciated in anyone and for anyone.

The third action is called the calmness of mind. I believe that after the second action, you naturally tend to head towards this direction because at this point, you start getting an idea of the value of serenity and harmony in your mind. I remember one ancient book referred to it as one of the beautiful jewels of wisdom. Calmness of mind is the result of long and patient self-control. In no way I am telling you that I have full control of my mind but, through meditation, I can get the feeling of its immensity. There is nothing as spectacular as having just a slight flash feeling of the emptiness in your mind.

As in meditation, I used to find a quiet place and dedicated ten or fifteen minutes maximum to shut all my thoughts down and calm my mind. I can honestly tell you that the most difficult part of this is to find the time to do it during your busy day; and even if you find the time, the hardest part of all is to convince your mind that you are not wasting your time, even if you cannot get rid of your thoughts and your mind keeps wandering.

I was absolutely convinced that achievement in general was the result of effort and thought. In fact, I started to understand how I evolved as a human being due to my thoughts. I discovered, understood and accepted that I was fundamentally the result of my thoughts. Am I getting too deep in psychology? I do not know, but what I do know is that if I am the result of my thoughts, everyone else is as well. Since then, in order to build true relationships, I understand others as a result of their thoughts.

I made the effort to understand more and more clearly the internal relations of things by the actions of cause and effect and with this understanding I made daily progress towards the calmness of my mind. My friends and some of my colleagues started noticing how I was becoming more able to adapt to others, more serene, more tranquil and I felt some of them were now more open to listening and learning from me. But I have to be honest and warn you that this strength and these small changes were developed with a lot of effort, practice and patience and not judgement, worries or complaints when I felt I was not making progress. I learned to enjoy the activity and though I failed and keep failing and I do not know if I will ever achieve the wonders of total serenity, it is also compensated with the strength of perseverance and character I am gaining that will help me to continue or start again every time I fail.

So you must start exercise yourself and adding effort to effort, patience to patience and strength to strength and never cease to develop. This is the only way I know to self control and true concentration of thoughts.

The final action I took to train my mind was to record my own voice on my phone saying positive affirmations, and I also download some inspiring positive affirmation recordings so I could keep my mind busy. During those days you would have seen me every day during my commute to work wearing my headphones and totally focused on listening. The result was so good that I still sometimes listen to them. I found two big advantages from these techniques and each of them opened a conversation for other important topics.

What I realised is that yes, my mind was busy, or distracted, or focused (whatever you want to call it) during the time I was listening. That not only considerably reduced the amount of negative thoughts, but the positive ideas from the recording were getting in my mind so deeply that by the time I arrived to work or home, I felt in an extraordinary mood so that most words that came out of my mouth were injected with a lot of energy and positivism.

Giving this initial result, I downloaded more recordings to my phone and I started feeling much better as I basically shut my ears to the "negative world" at least for a couple of hours a day.

Every day I was also reading the newspapers (and this is the second thing I realised) and after I read all the bad news, my mind remained with sad and negative feelings because I was entertaining all those negatives words and images in my mind, so I ended up being full of negativity and fear every day, early in the morning and right before going to work.

The issue here is that these negative thoughts create strong negative feelings in ourselves, which end up becoming beliefs. This is terrible! No need to say that from that day, I pretty much reduced my time reading newspapers to nearly zero. This was one of the best decisions ever in my life. It really had a strong positive impact on my mind, particularly because it changed the way I see the world and others. I shut down my eyes to that manipulated perception of the world that someone else want me to believe. It truly put me in a different position or perspective. While everyone else was trying to share or discuss or even convince others about negative news or opinions, I was the one who always had the good news to share, the different opinion to present to others, and naturally it was all adding towards the achievement of my vision.

Now you probably realised that I was taking control of something I definitely could control, my senses! And the reason I was doing it was because I realised that our thoughts are fed through our senses and those thoughts create our feelings. When I was looking for answers about how to control my thoughts, I learned that most of the knowledge we gain is through our senses.

However, we cannot be aware of our mind (through the normal senses) unless we commune with it. Our mind grows through the information it receives from our senses. So senses are fundamental to the development of the mind, but more important are the things presented to our senses. Again, this is extremely important because these impressions enter to our brain and become our thoughts and ideas behind our conversation and our actions. These impressions disappear but they leave images behind in our mind, which means the impression of the sense now becomes a quality of our mind. I hope you realise the importance of this statement. You have a tremendous power to change an impression (image) of the external into a quality of the mind. So a great starting point to control your thoughts is simply to develop supreme control over your senses.

This is a game and we can change the whole thing. So the game is very simple: first, we control what we see, what we hear, smell and touch, everything you sense will enter your mind, so you better make sure that those things are good. That's the reason why I do not watch any negative things, bad news or information and I do not hear any negative criticism. I don't accept it if it is not constructive. I immediately stop and reject it. Now that you have the knowledge of it and you are conscious about it, start training your mind to stop all that too; filter what enters your mind, be aware of any negative comment and reject it, but also be attentive to good comments and accept them. Here, we are trying to avoid creating more negative beliefs. Soon you will start to have control over your senses and you will notice great benefits.

But, as I said, it is only part of it. We are keeping the mind distracted, which is good and liberating, however it does not necessarily create that belief and faith that we are looking for simply because it doesn't completely remove the old negative thoughts we keep in our mind that cause those negative beliefs that are rooted in our conscious. Therefore, we need another part. That other part is related to what, in my opinion, is one of the greatest mysteries of human beings: consciousness. I truly believe that the knowledge I gained on consciousness and the way it works was one of the most important elements that helped me to become successful in the achievement of my definite purpose.

Let's forget for a moment about your thoughts and try to understand your belief system and the way it affects your goals and opportunities for growth. I remember I once saw an opportunity to speak at a local gig, but as soon as I start thinking about it, my limiting belief became stronger, making me feel that I was not that good, I was not prepared to speak, my content wasn't interesting...etc...so what would be my thought? Yes, I am not good enough for that, I cannot do it, so I did not take action and the opportunity was gone simply because I was not aware I had those negative beliefs in my subconscious mind affecting my thoughts, which then created my reaction, or lack of action to be precise.

BELIEFS SYSTEM

"Men often become what they believe themselves to be. If I believe I cannot do something, it makes me incapable of doing it. But when I believe I can, then I acquire the ability to do it even if I didn't have it in the beginning"

-Mahatma Ghandi

Have you realised that most sportspeople, actors and actresses, singers and any other performer that are interviewed after a great success like winning a medal or an award, when they are asked what they attribute their success, they always respond, "You have to believe in yourself!" Obviously this cannot be a coincidence or a prepared speech for all of them, it's simply true. Why do not we seem to believe that? And why we do not believe in ourselves?

Those negative thoughts in our mind do not allow us to embed this idea and be fully convinced of it. Thus, in order to fully accept this idea in our mind and heart, we must get rid of those negative thoughts, and to do so, we must get rid of the real cause of these thoughts: we must change the belief that caused them.

I am going to quickly explain what I think is the most relevant information anyone should know about consciousness. The reason I am taking the time to explain this to you is because I believe consciousness is the most natural way to achieve success in a creative not a competitive way.

Many successful people have paid the price of success with extremely hard work and competition, but through the understanding of consciousness, the price of success is nothing less than joyful and gratifying work. Yes, still work, but there is a huge difference. Here you will use your knowledge of consciousness to create the conditions of your external world and creating your vision.

The reading of scientific or academic articles about our subconscious mind is highly recommended at this point as it will make it easier for you to understand and believe it.

When I first read Napoleon Hills' "Think and Grow Rich", it simply called my attention to the way he emphasised the importance of the subconscious mind for personal success. His book is based on his interviews with some of the most successful people in the world at that time (including businessmen such as Andrew Carnegie, Henry Ford; great inventors such as Thomas A. Edison and A. Grahambell and even a president of the United States). Then more research pointed me to many other authors who clearly confirmed this interesting relationship between our subconscious mind and our external condition, which can be success or failure.

To understand consciousness, we need to understand the relationship between the conscious and the subconscious but I won't bother you with much detail about it. All you really need to know is that your conscious mind generates your ideas and thoughts, but your thoughts are created not only by the images you perceive through your senses, but also by your beliefs established in your subconscious mind. Those are the ones we are interested in right now.

Beliefs are assumptions and convictions that are held to be true, by us, regarding ourselves, other people and the world. Next time you are having a conversation with someone, realise that this person will be talking either about themselves, about others or about the world. Most probably their conversation will be negative and possibly involve complaining about themselves, others or the world. If this is the case and you are listening and paying full attention to them, you will see what lies behind those words are thoughts filled with limiting beliefs such as there is no hope, everyone wants to take advantage, I am a loser, life is unfair, I am not lucky, the whole world is wrong, you name it! So now think about what sort of belief can be revealed by your words and your thoughts.

Based on our definite goal and having gone through the process of self-discovery, you are now at the stage where you can identify empowering beliefs and you will take actions to strengthen them or to install new ones and then explore limiting beliefs, which you will reframe or delete completely. This is a very conscious process, which can be shared with close people who can be helpful in identifying where your limiting beliefs are.

After I was very clear about my vision and who I wanted to be, my biggest challenge was to believe that I could ever become that. I dreamed big and I have a tremendously ambitious goal as my definite aim, thus to create a belief that I could actually achieve it wasn't a quick task but certainly one that contributed the most to my self-learning and self-development plan.

I knew that there was only one way to start and it was by changing my limiting beliefs. To change my limiting beliefs, I first had to identify them, know how they were created and then accept them. It is not easy and it is painful; our ego does not allow us and even resists accepting that we ourselves are the main cause of all our internal and external issues, situations or condition. This is a very important step, but for me, it's the main way to prove the opposite of our limiting beliefs.

In this part, I decided I would create a new opposing belief so I could convince my mind and proof that my old beliefs were wrong. There is only one way I know how to do this: by taking action and proving that limiting belief is wrong. Every time I had a chance, I took the little risk. I took small actions every time I could. However, it is not easy at the beginning to take action, so we need a mental technique to support it. The best mental technique I have used is repetition! And not so much verbally, as you might think, but mainly mentally thorough thoughts. Beliefs are created and strengthened by repetition.

I truly believe that repetition is a great technique that can be used in conjunction with other methods to convince the subconscious mind to accept a new belief. For example, to improve my confidence, I knew I had to take small actions that evidenced I was increasing this personal quality. However, how I was going to take action if I was feeling unconfident? In my case, it was different, I guess. I had already gone through the self-awareness process and had a clear purpose, a focused vision and good knowledge of my strengths. I was already well ahead in the process of gaining full confidence. Yes, I needed to take some action to become fully confident, but first my priority was to keep the confidence I had gained, and I wanted to reinforce the message in my subconscious mind. Therefore, I did the opposite; I use repetitions, first to reinforce the message and then to gain strength to take some small actions. Thus, I repeated to myself (self-talking) every day that I was becoming more confident. It was a permanent repetition that I still sometimes do automatically before talking to a large audience. I repeated it so much that I started feeling it. I saturated my subconscious mind with this affirmation so that it ended up accepting it since I started believing it. In fact, what happened was that I was not giving my mind time to think the opposite, that I was not confident.

The reality is that those two thoughts cannot exist together in your mind. A positive and a negative thought cannot co-occur at the same time in the mind; they fight and the strongest one will win (Jim Rohn called it the battle in the mind).

This was very powerful for me and helped me to take action. I was feeling able to take the risk and I was willing to do it. Of course, every time I took a risk and successfully tested my confidence, I was adding evidence against my limited belief. I was conscious of my little success, I shared them with others and I celebrated them to create more impact in my subconscious mind.

The not so good news is that most of the time, the negative thought will win. Why? Well normally it carries more feelings with it. The thought with the strongest feeling will predominate in your mind. Here we go again, a new concept that triggered more research.

So previously the idea was to focus on improving the quality of our thoughts at all times. We now know that this is not easy as we need to keep control of our senses. But that is not all and it is a bit more complicated than that. So we learned about how our mind works and how we could possibly and consciously influence it. That is why we ended up learning about the conscious and subconscious mind and how they deal with thoughts and beliefs. We just learned the important role of feelings.

The relationship between these three aspects was fascinating for me and to understand it really changes our perspective from passively waiting to reach our destination to proactively enjoying life or honouring our existence by living and enjoying our journey to our destination. Thoughts help us to keep our vision close at all times, but it is feelings that create the right state of mind for us while we are in our journey. It is how you feel every instant of your life and what truly determines a successful life.

The Principles

What is your life philosophy? Do you live by following some sort of principle?

For many years, I lived with no particular philosophy or life principles. I had my values and certainly they were influencing the most important decisions and actions in my life. At a mental level, I always thought it was important to have a clear life philosophy. After all, many "successful" people have and recommend having it. However, I guess I never had time to think about it calmly and really I wasn't planning to sit and write one down and start living it.

Surprisingly, the opposite occurred. After so many years developing myself and growing as a human being, and as I started focusing more on my mindset ensuring that I have the right belief system, I ended up with a set of principles that pretty much regulate all my decisions, behaviour and actions as they are all related to the achievement of my definite purpose in live. I consciously created them. They are the result of my self-discovery, thus, my mindset is now my greatest asset. It simplified my decision-making process as I now consider that most of my decisions are right decisions since they are in line with my life purpose. Any decision that brings me closer to my definite purpose, even just a little bit, is a good decision for me and if they do not, at least I know they were authentic.

As my principles are tied to my values and those values are the result of a conscious understanding of my true self, which involves my soul, my heart, my mind and body, I truly believe that those decisions are not only right for me but also for those who I have contact with, like relatives, friends, colleagues or staff.

I have formed my principles or fundamental beliefs in three different areas related to the world, to myself and to others. These are the first set of beliefs that we need to review and change if needed. The basic beliefs in these three areas must be positive. Period. You must think positively about the world, about others and you must think positive about yourself overall. Every day, you must spend a few minutes meditating, thinking or at least reflecting on your own basic beliefs. Work on them, build them to be positive and strong.

Some of my principles or beliefs about the world that are now part of my mindset and determine the foundation for making any decision or taking any action are:

Abundance: We live in a world of abundance. There is unlimited wealth and unlimited opportunities for everyone. So don't worry about whether you can succeed in something, just focus on how to succeed in it. See our world: the oceans have unlimited resources, we do not even know how many minerals, animals and other resources our planet possesses, it is in constant creation and evolution; to think about scarcity is ridiculous. The world cannot change until you change your conception of it.

Create do not compete: It's not about choosing Option A or Option B. It's about Option C – an option you create which has everything you want, and more. The only competition you have is yourself.

Happiness: is the result of doing what brings you joy every day, every hour, every minute, in every action. It is not a goal to be achieved. I do what makes me happy and I do everything possible to avoid any other activity.

Success: is attaining the greatest possible height in body, soul, heart and mind development. It is making progress towards a consciously selected and clearly defined life purpose. It is the fulfilment of our potential; it is the mastery of our state of being.

Attachment: only causes suffering in the long run because nothing is permanent in this world. Don't mourn over the loss of something, be certain something better is coming if you are ready.

Failure: is a necessary part of success, it is simply a part of life's journey. Every great success is almost always preceded by a great failure. It's more important that you learn from your failure(s) and harness the lesson(s) so you can achieve your next success.

My principles or beliefs about myself:

Choice: Life is an experience that you actively create, not something you wait around to "happen". No matter how things may seem, you always have a choice. Only by accepting responsibility for that can you finally progress toward what you want.

Responsibility: Nobody is responsible for your life. You are. You are the only one responsible for your life. If you don't take responsibility for your life, no one will. The day you stop pushing blame onto others is the day your life is going to turn around. Remember, whenever you point a finger at someone else, there are three fingers pointing back at you.

Growth: Always challenge yourself to reach greater heights. There is always room to be better, regardless of who you are or what you have done. Be attached to the notion of growth, not an end state. Be committed to self-learning every day for the rest of your life.

Patience: Change that lasts: It's better to create sustainable change than change that is quick but does not last. Stop going for the easy way out. Learn how to create lasting change instead.

Limits: The only limit in life is you. No one's stopping you from becoming better and achieving more except yourself. To reach greater heights, identify your limits and remove them accordingly.

Fear: is a disempowering emotion to live with. Your real self is not filled with fear. Discard it and you will be set free.

My principles and beliefs about others:

People: Everyone is good. Even if they act wrongly, their nature is good. The nastiest of people are also the unhappiest of people. Be

114

kind to them because they are the ones who need your love the most. As a leader, to truly help your company, you must understand that your people are more important than the actual company.

Changing people: You can't change other people. You can only change yourself.

Respect: Everyone, no matter who they are, deserves respect. If you want others to respect you, it's important you respect them first.

Motivation: comes naturally when you do what you love. Think about this when trying to motivate or influence someone else.

Low consciousness people, #2: Low consciousness people hold you back from reaching greater heights. These include energy vampires, critical people, dishonest characters and people with temperament issues. Let them go from your life and send them love as you do that.

FEELINGS

"A positive attitude causes a chain reaction
of positive thoughts, events and outcomes.
It is a catalyst and it sparks extraordinary results."

-Wade Boggs

So here it comes. Neville answers the question of why the negativity tends to win most of the time...he said that feelings are the secret. What happens is that you have so many feelings associated to your negative thought, and very little feeling associated with the positive repetition as this is a mental process. When you really feel that you are not confident, it is that feeling that eliminates the positive affirmation. So he said that what we really need to control is our feelings. Moods or feelings are very important and can affect any situation or relationship; sometimes a discouragement can cause a bad mood and end up in failure. Therefore, we must learn to recognise a bad mood and also how to remove it and change it to a good one.

At this point, you probably think, this is driving me crazy! I kind of shared the same feeling at the beginning since I was trying to control my senses, my thoughts, beliefs, and now feelings, all at the same time in every single moment of every single day. I realised that perhaps it was easier to control the feelings. So what matters is how you feel every moment. However, this area is where we make the most mistakes as we allow external conditions to affect our mood and influence our feelings. Any person or situation can make us feel depressed or sad or inferior so now our fight is not against the thought, it's against inadequate feelings. You won't be able to remove it just by wishing it out, we must will it out. It means adopting another mood to take its place. The mastery of this process is to develop the ability to introduce or withdraw your moods at will (this is supreme self-control). We can will moods of happiness, courage, and confidence. The WILL can be made the master of all moods. (That's the reason why we have step three in our development process.)

I decided that at the beginning I would not fight negative thoughts and that I would focus on not allowing them to affect my feelings and change my mood instead. That was a bit easier for me. Indirectly and consciously, I was ensuring I felt good all the time. Can you imagine that? I was consciously ensuring that I was feeling good all the time! I was so determined to boost my mood that I would not allow any person or anything to affect me. So to have more days full of great moments and good feelings, I do this every day:

First of all, when I wake up, but still in bed, I consciously make the effort to feel happy and be in a good mood. Nothing else really matters in that moment. I just know I must be happy and I start my morning routine with a smile. It doesn't matter what my condition is at that time; even if I wake up feeling sick, I still make the effort to feel good. And the reason I can do that is because I learned, understood and I believed that I am not just my body; I am also my mind, my spirit and my heart. If a little part of my body is not good, the rest of me, my spirit, my heart and my mind are strong and I feel good because of it.

If you have consciously followed the first step explained in this book, this process is far easier than it seems. Your life purpose, your definite vision and your life plan will come to the rescue every time.

With the smile on my lips, I practice gratitude, I thank universe for my life, my health, for who I am, for what I do and for what I have. Then, I condition my mind. I dedicate an instant to know how I want to feel that day; I imagine how it is going to feel. I feel it first. With that clarity, I focus on the best of each experience and I remain alert of any negative thoughts that could affect the way I want to feel. Period.

The next couple of minutes I focus purely on my vision, my definite vision, and my goal. I simply contemplate it and use my imagination for a few minutes and entertain it so I create a long-lasting impression in my mind. I use this impression in my mind and recall it many times during the day. It keeps me focused and attentive. I know that is my purpose and whatever happens during the day, tomorrow I will still have to continue working for my definite vision.

From there, it is all about watchfulness! And of course, life challenges you every minute. In fact few minutes later, I normally start getting my first big challenges as soon as my little girls wake up, but I am alert and prepared, so I do not involve feelings or get emotional (not all the time, at least).

Then, when I am on the tube on my way to work, I remain alert of my mood and even later I become aware of how easily other people get affected and their mood changes when they have a little argument about who took the first seat on the train, or who pushed them or touched them, or another million things that make them change their mood so early in the morning. They cannot control it and end up with feelings of anger or frustration. This awareness of the whole situation helped me to develop loving compassion for most people.

You will witnesses exactly the same situation at work. People and the environment will try to affect your mood. In the beginning, just to arrive to the office was making me feel very uncomfortable and frustrated, but later I started managing it and I did not allow this feeling to take over me again. It was not easy to deal with it but I overcame those negative feelings through the continued use of different mental strategies and techniques that I will explain in the next chapter.

After work and in the evening, I still keep mindful of any external condition or other people that could affect my mood. In the evening just before going to bed, I prepare and condition my mind during the evening routine for the following day. I will explain this in more detail in the following section.

The learning lesson here is this: if we realise in advance that the mind and will and can always find a way to handle irritation, fear, worry, etc., we can protect ourselves before getting into any disturbing situation. We must allow time to reflect before getting emotional.

Remember, it is all self-development and this you can do it. Practice makes the will stronger. In the beginning, it will be difficult, but after that, it will become easier.

MENTAL STRATEGIES
AND TECHNIQUES

"My last thought before I take the club away isn't a thought at all. It's a picture, a visualization, a sensation. If I think of swinging slowly, my last thought isn't "swing slowly." It's an image of me swinging slowly."

-Jack Nicklaus

In the previous chapter, you noticed I constantly refer to some mental strategies or techniques I have used during my personal development. They are basic tools that we must use to secure the success of our journey, which is the daily fulfilment of our purpose and the continuous personal growth that would take us to become the person we want to be.

I personally use them on a daily basis to keep me focused on my vision, to keep my mind in a state of faith and belief and also as a quick "pick me up" motivation strategy in really hard situations, when nothing seems to work in my favour.

I use mainly three types of techniques: visuals, auditory and self-talk.

Visualisation

My first degree is a BA (Hons) in industrial design. The reason I got into that was because I love drawing very much and I was really good at it (not so much nowadays…). However, a few years after I graduated and worked on it for a couple of years, I regretted studying that profession. I thought I kind of wasted my time since I learned very little "important knowledge" and developed only a few so-called hard skills that were key to find a traditional good job. However, I later realised that in that career, I developed an amazing skill that is extremely important in personal success.

During five years in a module called Taller, I learned the whole process of how you create something from nothing (in this case, a product). This is to take an idea, which in theory is nothing, and convert it into something tangible. This process has several steps, most of them very rational, very logical steps; however, there were two steps in the middle of the process which I never felt comfortable about - they were weird...too weird for me, at least. In short, the process begins with finding a need in the market that requires not just a new product but an innovative one. You do research, analyse the situation, look at current solutions or alternatives and them it comes "the black hole", the "creative part" where you had to somehow get the inspiration for a solution and design your product, then build the prototype or model, test it and send to production.

Many year later, I realised that "the black hole", the "creative part" required me to apply the right use of the faculty of imagination. Moreover, I had to use one of the most popular mental strategies, visualisation. Basically, before you can ever touch a product, it has to be created in the mind of the creator. This is the creation process; nothing can be been created if it does not first exist in the mind of its creator. Exactly the same happens with your definite vision. It cannot and it will not be a reality if you do not visualise it first in your mind. This mental strategy is very popular in sport psychology, particularly in golf psychology.

At the very beginning, as soon as I created my vision and did my life planning mind-map, I looked for an app on my mobile phone and created that mind-map with the idea of using it to constantly remind me about my goals.

Later, I decided to move it to the Evernote app, where I could also write my statements of purpose and include some pictures related to my personal vision. Together, these three elements became my home and daily bread. I felt reconnected every time I looked at it. It gave me the energy to act and the perseverance to continue working towards my ultimate vision. I truly felt like never giving up before I achieved it. As of 2012, I included short-term, midterm and long-term goals in my life plan mind map. I have already achieved many big goals. I never lose focus of them. It is my daily activity to look at it, reflect on it and plan my day accordingly.

Towards the end of 2012, I took it further. I wanted it to be more inspiring and motivational so I decided to create a video about my purpose and my vision and uploaded on the Internet for my personal use so I could watch it anytime I felt the need.

Auditory

The second mental strategy I use, although it is perhaps the most important one for me, is auditory. Since 2012, I have listened to my own positive affirmation recording on my mobile phone daily. I listen to it in the morning and also in the evening. When I am travelling, I mostly listen to TED talks and motivational videos. Right now and every time I am writing or working, I listen to the music that uses a prevailing isochronic tone of 7.5Hz, which is associated with inter-awareness of self and purpose and I feel I can focus and concentrate faster and easier. If I am resting, I use music with Alpha waves, which are linked to relaxation, positive thinking, self-growth, problem solving, imagination, stress reduction, mood elevation.

Perhaps the most important method I use is mind programming when I am sleeping. I have been doing it almost every night since 2013. I created a YouTube channel and have a selection of videos that have binaural beats to programme the subconscious mind and I like to listen to a bit of everything, from relaxation and gratitude to super learning and memory improvement.

Self-Talk and Autosuggestion

Dr. Shad Helmstetter in his book "What To Say When You Talk To Yourself" wrote that "the brain simply believes what you tell it the most, and it doesn't matter if we believed or not and it doesn't care if it is right or wrong."

I cannot prove it, but I certainly believe that if we do this, it is half of our success. Recognize and cultivate the power of autosuggestion. It works and is an essential tool in maintaining peak performance. We are all performers in one way or another and it is particularly valuable to use such techniques with athletes and public figures for our own enhancement. If you want to become more enthusiastic, repeat "I am more enthusiastic today and am improving this trait daily." Repeat it over and over. Buy a little notepad and write out this mantra 500 times. Do it for three weeks with regular practice and feel that this quality is developing. Very soon it will come. This is a strategy that Indian sages have employed for thousands of years to aid their spiritual and mental development. Do not be discouraged if the results are not immediate, they will certainly develop. The spoken word is a powerful influencer of the mind.

Chapter 5.

HABIT CREATION

"Men's natures are alike; it is their habits that separate them."

-Confucius

HABITS

Habits, as explained previously in the mindset effect section, are highly influenced and are basically the result of your mindset first, then your mental attitude. They are very important because they are the behaviours and the source of progressive activity and the degree of our achievement depends upon our degree of progressive activity. I want to make sure you are clear about this: progressive activity does not depend on the amount of work that is done, but is based on the amount of work done by the worker for his advancement.

Lack of clarity in this little detail is what was affecting me and is still affecting most workers, professionals and leaders in the world. Ask anyone how hard they work, and most of them will answer "very hard", but still you see they are not successful. The reason is that they work hard to get their work done, which is good, but they do not work hard on their advancement or personal growth. Good habits create progressive activity and you can become more active or very passive depending on your habits. In fact, passiveness and activeness become habits. So you are either an active person or a passive one. The first and hardest step to become an active person is to master ourselves. That accomplished, we can control and lead others.

From the first step of your journey, when you gained knowledge of your qualities and your values, you strengthened your character and continued to become a person of principles. You are active with honesty, you think and act right, your achievement comes through the right methods.

Even though the active process can be slow at times, it surely will bring results. Personally for me, the most important advantage is that I am truly being active, not only for the financial reward but for the joy of being active as part of my self-development. From my mindset and mental attitude, I have easily created many physical habits, which I have pretty much standardised.

Although, our personal development process involves the improvement of the body, which naturally includes exercising, eating, sleeping and even breathing, being active does not refer to physical, but to mental activities. For this reason, I will say that you should find the easiest, quickest and most efficient way to do your duties. It will make your work nearly as automatic as possible through the formation of efficient habits.

Our mental habits, on the other hand, are far more important. The key here is to understand that this idea as a concept is very simple but its application is really hard: habits are conditions under our control. It is incredible how we allow terrible habits to control our life and we seem to be incapable of changing them as if they rule our world. I can't believe how many people define themselves in a negative way because of bad habits and they hide behind the sentence *"I am like that...and there is nothing I can do about it."*

How many times do you blame your country of origin or your culture for one of your bad habits: *"I am from x country...that's why I am always late...we are like that..."* Isn't it incredible? A bad habit is controlling you and there is nothing you can do...right! You don't achieve any result, but of course it is not our fault, we are just like that.

Once again, habits are conditions under our control and if you have the desire and the will, you can change old habits and create new ones. The mental training we are going through makes this process far easier as you change from one day to other.

Follow the steps described in this book and you will became a very active person, which is one of the traits of successful people; thinking right and being right is not enough, you need to be active. Take all this knowledge and apply it so you start creating the mental habits you need.

MENTAL HABITS

"All the problems of the world could be settled easily if men were only willing to think. The trouble is that men very often resort to all sorts of devices in order not to think, because thinking is such hard work."

-Thomas J. Watson

In this process of developing a strong and positive mental attitude, I have taken you through what I know and experienced as the key elements to build the right mindset. Although I have been giving you personal examples obviously based on my own experience, it has been always from the perspective of illustrating the theory. However, I have discussed very little about what was actually happening in my daily activity when I was applying all these ideas.

During the last four, nearly five, years, I have changed and created many habits, some of them voluntarily and some others totally involuntarily but they are all a result of my journey. So below are pretty much some of the life-changing habits that you are about to create in a natural way.

THE HABIT OF SEEING VALUE IN WHAT WE DO

After working hard on self-awareness, and dedicating time to create my personal and definite vision, I started creating what I think was my first new mental habit in this journey: the habit of seeing value in everything I do, particularly the value of my goals and possibilities as well as all the benefits they would bring to my life.

Seeing the value of my vision persuaded me to abandon the sort of life I was living for more than 30 years, and I committed to create my future. Seeing the value of my vision filled me with determination to take action. Constant appreciation of the value of my definite dream made me believe I could achieve it. I started visualising it more and more. Little did I know at that time that I was influencing my subconscious mind through conscious repetition. I was creating the belief and an unwavering faith that I could achieve it, and equally important, I was creating a strong appetite for new knowledge.

THE HABIT OF CONTEMPLATION AND VISUALISATION

At a mental level, I was determined to live my dream, so I started creating the right conditions for my new purpose and vision. Day by day, I was developing the habits of contemplating and visualising my definite vision. I was cherishing my purpose, the charm of my new thoughts, the feelings and emotions that came every time my imagination presented me with an image of those dreams in my mind. I consciously dedicated more and more time every day to contemplate and nurture it as I was already convinced that my future conditions would grow from this.

Since then, the belief that it was all possible for me never stopped growing and it was all because of this new mental habit I developed voluntarily. It only depended on my own capacity. Nothing else.

Constant contemplation of my vision helped to strengthen my desire for the achievement of my goal. It was all about creating that feeling that Napoleon Hill calls a "burning desire" that became directly responsible for millions of success stories around the world. At this moment, the idea that I could control my own future and direct all my thoughts and actions towards the achievement of my vision was becoming very strong and dominant. A few months later (not days or weeks...), the first positive results were already presenting themselves in front of me and I realised that it wasn't by chance or by luck, it was a lot of mental effort and continuous action towards the achievement of that vision.

THE HABIT OF SELF-LEARNING

So much thinking about my vision became an obsession for me to find ways or plans to make it a reality. This increasing desire for new ideas and knowledge made me get into the habit of researching and from there into permanent reading. At one point I was carrying at least three books with me everywhere I went. Reading has become my favourite hobby and gaining knowledge on how to achieve my vision is always my obsession.

I began to watch videos of interviews, TED talks and documentaries about personal development. I subscribed to audiobooks, so I could learn more on the go rather than simply listening to music. I very frequently registered for selected webinars and online courses in order to learn more and more and I participated in live conferences in order to stay updated with the latest developments in terms of personal growth, success, leadership and entrepreneurship. And I have been spending at least ten hours a week at the British Library for the last five years.

At this point, you probably realise that I had no time for anything else, so obviously I became desperate for time! I recognised the value of time and committed to achieving financial independence in order to avoid trading time for money. I was mentally and consciously aware that time had much more value than money. That was a huge realisation for me. Most of us know the value of time, yet we still live our lives by trading it for money. We know it but we do nothing about it. The reason is that we are not convinced of its value; if we were fully convinced of the value of time, we wouldn't be spending our time in jobs or activities that we do not want to do or that we do not love. I became extremely careful with my time and the way I use it.

For instance, the time I used to watch TV naturally decreased, less and less until it was reduced to nearly none. I felt I lost interest in it and I had so much to learn that it became a waste of time for me, until one day we moved home and decided to leave all TV sets behind in the old house.

THE HABIT OF WATCHFULNESS (The Vigilant Mind)

Similarly, anything else that was not related to the true purpose of my life and my vision became irrelevant. Daily news, including newspapers, radio, magazines, etc. and particularly those that were negative were also quickly out of my normal day. I became very conscious about what I was allowing into my mind. I never ever read about violence, crimes, crises, etc. again. People kept asking me how could I possibly live without news, and I always answered the same: if a particular piece of news was very important, I knew everyone would comment on it anyway, be it on the train, in the office, in the supermarket, anywhere. This is a great advantage for the development process of a leader as you suddenly stop seeing the world as the worst place to be in and your mind shifts to a feeling that is more in harmony to perceive the good and the abundance of the universe. This also helps to clear your mind of all those irrelevant thoughts that stick with you the whole day after reading or watching the morning news even before starting your day.

I noticed how my change in mindset was already having a positive impact on my habits and behaviour. It was extremely motivating. Since you are a child, your parents and every adult tells you about what a negative habit watching frequently TV is. Still even if you tried hard, you found it very difficult to stop, right? Or how hard is to get into the habit of reading when you are not used to it? Nearly impossible! But now I was just changing my habits for new ones as easily as brushing my teeth.

Unfortunately, I had to let go of old friendships since my interests changed completely and some of them reacted to my changes. I had to sacrifice them as I could no longer spend much time with them. On the other hand, I was willing to meet new like-minded people in order to learn more and share my experience. These were all important changes for me, but above all, I felt my new thinking habits were the most essential ones and where I noticed the most change. This is funny, my friends and colleagues started recognising me as the "positive mentality guy" and guess what? I began to think, talk and act like that.

THE HABIT OF CARING AND NURTURING MY BODY, SOUL, MIND AND HEART.

With all these changes in habits, I had to plan and reorganise my daily schedule so I could include all the new activities I wanted to do in my life and remove all the time-wasting activities I did not want in my life anymore. I set a routine, including tasks for my body such as breathing exercises, drinking more water, healthy eating and a routine to sleep better and feel energized; other tasks for my soul and heart included meditation, silent time and retreats and also some activities for my mind, such as reading, learning and writing. My personal self-development was now well on its way to change my whole way of living. It was the result of the new beliefs and the new mindset I was building.

The more I read, listened, watched and researched, the more knowledge I attained and the more I wanted to know. As my self-knowledge grew, my beliefs changed and so did my habits. I am gaining the ability to think, speak and act with a humble mind that is filled with great determination to help others as my purpose and to the achievement of my definite goal; I am convinced that I am gaining the ability to merit my vision.

THE HABIT OF PERMANENCE

As there is no teaching, idea, method or philosophy that wakes you every morning and reminds you to take action or apply what you learned, I created some routines and rather than trying to manage my time to do a lot of things (which is kind of weird, how can we possibly manage something like time?), I focused on mind management.

To make sure I will never stop learning in my life, I have created a few daily routines and I embed self-learning as a compulsory activity in them. I first dreamed about what a perfect day for me would be like: I visualised every aspect of it, the time I wanted to wake up every day, the place and the environment I wanted to be in, all the activities I wanted to do and the people I wanted to share it with, the feelings I wanted to experience, the emotions, and the general mental state I wanted to have, the sort of work I wanted to do and the conditions I wanted to do that work in, the type of food and everything else I could include in there. I designed this day and from it I created some daily mental routines that would help me to keep up with my personal growth day by day. Out of all this, I finally created a yearly calendar to have a visual support.

My morning routine, for instance, included to wake up with a smile, a few minutes of mind-conditioning followed by a breathing exercise during 5 minutes of finger tapping, a two minute gratitude session, then I have a glass of water or two with lemon followed by fifteen minutes of morning meditation, a five minute intensive stretching exercise, one minute to read my personal statement purpose, five minutes listening to some positive affirmation and finish with a short motivating self-talk. Then I am ready to start a magnificent day.

Here you begin unfolding your own deepest being; you are gathering together the various threads of your nature and weaving them whole; you are now beginning to feel that life is worth living; the conviction is rising in you that your life need not be a mere weary repetition like that of a horse in a thrashing machine turning round and round in the same place; you will come to know in your own deepest soul; that you are creating and moulding that soul of yours. It makes you a person of honour and you bring joy to those who are near to you. The influence goes beyond the family circle; it extends to the village, the town, the country.

In Part 2, we have created the conviction and the belief that you will achieve and you will work towards that. When you have created these beliefs, you will go and work in a completely different state. After this, I went to work full of enthusiasm and energy and motivation and I saw how my colleagues, who were doing exactly the same job, still felt depressed, frustrated, tired and stressed. And I can tell you that the difference between my happiness and their depression was my purpose and my mental attitude. Since that moment, I believed I was following my purpose and, sooner or later, it would take me to my vision. It was just a matter of time. I knew that was the beginning and that would not matter because I was working for something bigger. I knew the time would come when I would be travelling around the world giving my talks and doing what I love. That's what kept me waking up early and going to work happily and coming back home with satisfaction. That's what purpose and a positive mental attitude did for me. If you're currently working and you do not feel good about it, you are simply not satisfied because you have not found your purpose. This is sad because you might be suffering and the worst thing is that it might even be a good job, with a nice environment and nice people and it might be a dream job for many people, but it is still a pity you are not enjoying it because you have not found your purpose.

END OF PART TWO.

PART 3.
BECOME SUCCESSFUL

STEP 3. ATTAIN THE ENERGY

Ch. 6. This third step explains where the process of doing things begins. It tells us about "the power" and helps us understand what that power is – the power that enters our consciousness; the power that is directed by our mind and controlled by the will; and will eventually make us do anything. It describes the process we need to follow in order to attain, increase and benefit from it. Finally, it also explains the concept of desire and its significance in filling the mind with determination and securing success.

Ch. 7. This chapter focuses on taking actions towards your definite goal. It tells about the way to create the spirit to take immediate actions by explaining how to first get that spirit before engaging in any action. It describes the seven elements that are necessary to turn every single action you take into an act of excellence by applying all the concepts learnt in previous chapters.

Chapter 6.

POWER

"Knowledge is not a passion from without the mind,
but an active exertion of the inward strength,
vigor and power of the mind, displaying itself
from within."

-Ralph Cudworth

POWER AND DESIRE

"A small body of determined spirits fired by an unquenchable faith in their mission can alter the course of history."

-Mahatma Gandhi

If we would do anything, we must have a conception of the thing to be done (your vision), and then follow it up by a decisive reason for doing it (your purpose), and we do it by the power (the desire) which is born with our decisive reason.

This last point, the responsibility for the actual action, is the one I would like to introduce or present to you as the third and fundamental step to the process of becoming a person with the ability to achieve your vision.

This step is as important as each of the other two for the successful achievement of your definite goal. Ignoring one of these steps would surely lead to your failure. You might achieve your goal, but you are not likely to have the joyful journey we have been discussing in this book. You might have a clear vision of your future and a noble purpose to achieve it, a strong mental attitude, and still you might simply not have the spirit to take action on it.

There are a couple of things I would like you to keep in mind before I start talking about this: The fact that I am referring to it as step three does not necessarily mean that it is the final step out of the three; remember they are all fundamental and ideally you should make progress in each of them from the very beginning.

The second point I would like to emphasise here (once again) is to keep your open mind! This isn't an easy topic people talk about on a daily basis. In fact, you hardly hear about it in any formal or informal educational context. How many times do you see a module or a course at university dedicated to the will or any related concept?

Thirdly, I will refer to it as "power" or "energy", meaning exactly the same force, that impulse that comes from inside and brings the energy or the courage to produce the action.

Finally, I am talking from my own experience, my research, my deep reflection and my understanding of what I believe is one of those mysteries of our human nature that we have mostly neglected to discover or understand, let alone to use or apply it. I first learned what I know of this topic back in 2013 from a collection of books written by different authors between 1890 and 1909 held at some US and British university libraries.

It caught my attention simply because when I started teaching my personal development process to other people, I noticed that even though they knew what they wanted, and they had high levels of self-awareness and self-knowledge, they had to try really hard to take action towards their goal, so they saw no progress. This was shocking for me because, personally, I still have exactly the same strong energy pushing me every single day to make progress in every aspect of my life towards my definite vision. I say it was shocking because I was convinced that my energy, will, courage, power, was coming from the same source: my purpose and vision. Well, clearly it was not. Then, I thought maybe it was because I have more ambition and determination, or I was desperate to move away from my current situation, so that is why I have so much of this force. Again, that was just my theory, but I still wanted to understand what was really happening. The truth is that I didn't know where to start. How could I start if I didn't even know what I was looking for? Still, I decided to go further in understanding the nearly impossible to understand: where the process of doing things really begins…

One Sunday morning after nearly 5 days lecturing my then 7-year-old daughter about will power and how she could use it so she could get the impulse and jump into the pool from a two-meter high trampoline, I realised there was something else needed other than just willpower if we wanted to take action. She was capable of doing it, as she had been swimming since she was five; she was willing to it, as she told me a few times she really wanted to do it and was looking forward to do it. She had the desire and confidently walked to the trampoline. She queued behind other children who were also doing it. She saw that they could do it and she told me that if they could do it, surely she could do it. It was her turn and she went up to the edge of the trampoline, raised her hands, closed her eyes, and waited a couple of seconds. We were all cheering her on and were convinced it would be really fun for her as she really wanted to it. But, when she was ready to jump, she opened her eyes and looked down at the pool. At that moment, all her power to act disappeared immediately. She stood there for a good couple of seconds and really tried to do it. We could see her desperation, but still she couldn't do it. She came down feeling frustrated and, of course, the feeling of failure took over her. So what happened? It took me a lot of thinking, reading and more research about this strange situation. When you have a clear goal, a definite purpose to realise it, the capabilities and the will to do it, you think you have everything to take action, but still you don't act. What element is still missing? Of course, I could not leave you here without this answer, since my biggest desire is for you to take action immediately on your personal development.

This is what I learned. I tested it and it works for me. Once again, I BELIEVED it, applied it and I consistently make progress towards my definite goal simply because it helps me to take action.

Many authors call this missing element "Power" and many other identify it as "Force". For me, it is simply that mysterious spark of energy that kicks us to act. I did not mind what it is called, what I cared about most was to understand what was it, how it works and if I could gain more of it. This is the natural element we humans have against procrastination; this power is something by which we act. However, the most important benefit of this power is that, as result of beating procrastination and getting things done, we are building character and increasing knowledge.

When I have been able to voluntarily direct this power, I managed to make huge steps. It helped me to consistently write my notes for the last 3 years, something that was very hard for me at the beginning. It has helped me to keep a strong habit of daily meditation so that even when I feel I cannot or when I am really tired, still this energy comes to my rescue. It helped me to develop my first leadership programme. It gave me the push to get accredited by an awarding organisation and gave me that extraordinary strength to travel and deliver my first course in Africa, all organised by myself with no experience in the market. This power come to my support every day and give me that spark of energy to sit down and write this book, and I can tell you, because of that power I am hundred percent convinced I will finish it.

The first characteristic of this power is that is spiritual, so we gain it, we cultivate it and we grow it through meditation. This energy is controlled by your will and you can apply it to physical or mental actions. A very easy example to recognise this force is early in the morning when your alarm clock goes off and you know you must wake up to do something that is really important for you. At that moment you have the desire to stand up, then your mind receives the energy and your own is what controls and selects what to you with it. If this energy is enough, you will stand up from your bed immediately and will go about your tasks. However, if this energy is not enough, that task certainly won't get done, at least not at that time. You can see this is all logical, real and it makes sense. I didn't waste time thinking about where this energy comes from as I think it is a useless discussion. I prefer to move into how we can obtain this energy.

Clearly we need it for every single action, no matter how big or small, and obviously, with or without understanding how to obtain this energy, you can get it as long as you have the will. However, it is much better for us to know how can we consciously get it. It is a natural and logical first step to desire this power. Isn't it the same with knowledge, for example? If you are interested in getting knowledge or increasing your knowledge, logically the first step is to desire it. I have no doubt about it. This step is so obvious that we forget about it, and we do not even care about it because we don't think it's necessary. Big mistake! What makes you think that you do not need to desire it? Or to ask for it? In fact, we constantly do this with other qualities of the mind. But what happens is we do it unconsciously and automatically, so we do not realise we are asking for things. For instance, don't you desire or ask for patience every time you are feeling frustrated with someone else's actions? Next question: Do you always get that energy?

By consciously desiring this energy, you can obtain it and direct it onto any physical or mental effort you select with your will. What I then learned is that the strength of this desire will determine the degree of power attained to achieve this mental and physical activity, an incredible idea presented back in 1913 by William R Ganson.

As he wrote in his book, "Success in Business", learning how to get power by desire requires practice. For me, that was the beginning. At the same time, I was gaining self-knowledge and creating my definite vision and I was trying hard to develop a strong desire for it so I would never give up on it.

I now have the ability to see how most people want the get rich quick solution in our culture these days but they do not desire it sufficiently to work for it. As soon as we see that there is sacrifice involved, we desist and stick to what we have.

How many people want to change their job yet don't do anything about it? They complain all day, every day but they do not have the required desire needed to take action. But of course, no one would accept this reality, we prefer other excuses, like "I need to pay my bills" or "I do not have time to look for something else", etc. But the real reason is they do not have enough power or desire to do it.

On the other hand, if you look at successful people, you see they desire and immediately work for it. Do something about it now. Even if it is a small step, it will create momentum and more desire to continue. Every time someone recommends me a book to read, which they know would be very useful for me or my business, I look for it immediately. I take my phone out, Google it and buy it straight away. This is how quick I learned to act, and there is no other reason apart from this power or energy that I desire so much. I desire to become a bestselling author to share these ideas all over the world; I desire it so much that I proceed systematically along the best lines to get the reward. I truly believe in it, I desire it faithfully and persistently.

As you are training your mind, remember to do the following every day with persistence and patience. If your desire is strong enough, you will always make progress towards your goal.

Building this desire is easier if you follow the visualisation technique described in a previous chapter. Every time you have a personal or professional, clear and specific goal, you must do this in addition to any process you currently follow to achieve your goals.

1. Every time I want to create a leadership event in Africa and before I take any single action towards it, I imagine and visualise it fully in my mind. I know how important is to visualise my goal, whatever is it. I see myself in the venue, I see the exact number of participants I want in the course and I try to see as many details as possible about the experience I want to have. I create an almost perfect image of my expected outcome. After this, I know exactly what I want with all the details. Then, I start working on what I need to make it happen. From that, I know what venues I need to contact and book, I know how many participants I want to have and how I can reach them, etc.

2. I keep this image in my mind and picture it as frequently as I can. You might see me eating or walking or doing something, but my mind is at work visualising myself already giving the training. It is impossible for me not to take constant action towards it. You now know I use any method to help me remember it: photos on my phone, or a mind map or videos.

3. I keep my mental state of believing at all times. Never allow doubts about its attainment.

4. Analyse the specific possibilities you have and then desire for the power to achieve the greatest possible success in each of these prospects individually. There must be a sufficient desire.

Remember, I am not asking you to change any procedure or strategy that you are currently using to achieve your personal and professional goals, I am suggesting you to do this as a complement to your current processes.

The purpose of following these steps is to provide the necessary power to accomplish not only the big goals but also the little tasks of our daily life which all lead to the definite goal or purpose. There are many small tasks every day that we postpone, simply because we do not have enough or sufficient desire to attain the power needed to do them. Procrastination is a term that really means "waiting for desire to strengthen".

I would like to close this section with a question: how many times have you postpones something that you really wanted or needed to do because you did not have enough desire to attain the power to do it?

DESIRE

*"The starting point of all achievement is the desire.
Keep this in mind all the time. Weak desires give
weak results, just as a small fire gives small heat"*

-Napoleon Hill.

You cannot express desire without a reason, thus it is necessary for you to have a reason for the desire. Now you probably understand why I decided that a clear personal development journey must start with a strong reason. This is the main cause of success and/or failure. Thus, our reason must be carefully chosen, taking everything into consideration but particularly with the fulfilment of our body, mind, heart and soul in mind. We must also take into consideration that the reason why you desire it so much is because it creates an extraordinary feeling of personal gratification.

You must firmly establish big enough goals in your mind to awaken strong and continuous desire. Greater goals produce greater desires. I cannot emphasise it enough. First, we must ensure this "reason" is desirable and is going to be desirable for the rest of our lives. It should not be something we know we will achieve in couple of years. That is why material things such as having a house or a luxury car produce a mere feeling of wishing but never a strong burning desire. When I was creating my definite personal vision, I moved away from the "having" or the "doing" things and moved more towards the "being", "becoming" and even "feeling" as the source of my personal vision. An exciting point to start for me was recommended by Jim Rohn in one of his conferences: "find a way to serve others".

Watchfulness and a vigilant mind are extremely important to avoid any negative thoughts that impact your desire. Feelings such as fear, worry, indifference, doubt, or any similar influence can reduce your desire considerably if they are present in your mind when you are expressing your desire.

Be alert to any sign of procrastination because it is an indication that your desire is not really strong enough, and that it is perhaps simply a feeling of hoping or wishing for something. When I first created my plan to achieve my definite goal, I included some goals to develop expertise in Neurolinguistic programming (NLP), but I realised that I was constantly postponing it and making excuses to avoid it. Obviously, my desire for it wasn't strong and I made very little progress so I reorganised my plan and removed this goal from it. It is fine to have some smaller goals that keep your desire strong, but you must only choose a definite overarching vision that requires all those goals and use your will to focus all your energy and your effort into achieving that vision. "The object is to want it so much and become so determined to have it that you convince yourself you will have it"; that was the best sentence I got from the book "Think and Grow Rich" by Napoleon Hill.

It is part of your self-development to increase your desire. Obviously, it takes time and persistence but by following the steps described in this book, I am convinced that you can definitely develop a strong desire for the achievement of your goal. Naturally, some of you might find this strange, or harder than others. I understand that but the key is once again persistence. You will see day by day or week by week that your desire grows and some days it happens so much and so fast that you can hardly keep up with your actions; you just want to do more and more towards your goals that you can hardly stop. Something I can confidently add is that even in the worst conditions with little support from others, you still feel like never giving up.

By now, you know the importance of desire in this process, and really this idea is "the one" to secure success. But there is one more thing I need to discuss here regarding of the three key areas in which you are going to use the your will to direct the power you get from your desire.

1. Attention

Use your will to determine what things you should focus your attention on. Or better, the power or energy you gain from your desire should be primarily used to keep your attention on things that are not just related to but are supportive of your goals. Keep alert of the things you observe. Remember your thoughts and beliefs are shaped by the information received through your senses. Do not focus so much on other people's daily problems if you do not have solutions for them. Always command your attention towards positive people and positive self-talk. Here you are gaining self-control of the senses. Finally, I would like to summarise this paragraph with one of my favourite lines from Wallace D. Wattles: "Use this energy to obligate yourself to think and do the right thing." I dream with leaders who have this mentality and work to develop the same mentality in their followers.

2. Concentration

When you have more control over your attention, you are obviously removing a lot of distraction and unnecessary thoughts from your mind. With this clearer mind, you can use some of the energy to concentrate purely on your goal. The less distraction, the purer the mind will become and the easier it is to concentrate constantly on what is important for you. Concentration must continue until you feel your mind is filled with determination. This is a vital characteristic of achievers, and you are in the process of becoming one of them. The more I practice concentration, the faster and the more power I receive to act.

3. Persistence

The third area where you want your will to direct your energy is persistence. It is not enough to appeal for power by training your mind occasionally. Persistence, continuity and discipline are absolutely necessary. This is the hardest part, and that is where you need a lot of energy. That is why creating a strong desire is crucial so you can never say you have enough desire. Every day, every moment, every action, every person can be a challenge and you must have the habit of working on your desire consciously and at stated periods, at least once a day. You must be proactive and prepared to deal with fear or worry whenever they arise in your mind.

I am now moving even closer to the moment or the minute or even the seconds before we actually take action.

Before starting any set task that is directly or indirectly related to your definite goal, be it a task to achieve a personal or professional, small or medium goal, you must remind your mind about its power to help you with the answer or best solution. Desire this power so your will can direct it to the task. This mental process is extremely beneficial any time you are ready to take an action, but particularly in those moments when you stand helpless before an obstacle. Think about this when you are in this situation and feel close to being defeated by procrastination or any other obstacle, as there is very little possibility of making progress with that state of mind.

You really need to act immediately and, as crazy as it might sound, you need to find a place to put yourself together where you can internalize the whole situation, focus your attention (close your eyes to avoid any distraction) and desire the power to accomplish whatever task you have set in mind (no wish but desire, strong desire!). It might take you a minute or 10 minutes, use whatever you need. This is an exercise of concentration where you remove everything from your mind by "will" and fully concentrate and focus all your attention upon your task. The desire has to be very strong and continuously in mind. Remain like that for as long as you feel that any fear or worry or confusion or even mental and physical tiredness disappear and you are ready to work on your task. When your mind is clear of fear or doubts, work that desire up until near fever heat to get the answer. This is a process of attention, concentration and action.

At this point, I concluded my longest research in this topic. I finally discovered how to create the "burning desire" that Napoleon Hill and many other contemporary authors made so popular as they referred to it as the starting point of all achievement.

Chapter 7.

PURE ACTION

"Action is the foundational key to all success."

-Pablo Picasso

ACTION

"I have been impressed with the urgency of doing.
Knowing is not enough; we must apply.
Being willing is not enough; we must do."

-Leonardo da Vinci

If you get perfect knowledge of everything you have read in this book up to here and do not take any action, obviously you won't achieve anything. You will stay right where you are and nothing, absolutely nothing will change. It is because knowledge is not power, the application of knowledge is.

On the other hand, ignore everything you have read so far in this book and just focus on doing something, anything, and you will achieve more. We do not know what you could possibly achieve but you will get something.

Neither situation is ideal. It is the combination of the knowledge and its application that will take you to the place you really want to be, and not just any place, but the one that was intended for you.

During many years, I worked hard on hundreds of projects from product design in the manufacturing sector, to managing people in the retail industry, to managing academic organisations, to directing my own organisation and even though I had great achievements, I never received so many professional compliments as I constantly receive now days. In every training, after talking consecutively for six hours each day, many of the participants come to me and ask me if I have always had the degree of confidence, strength, courage, forceful and spirit I demonstrate during the training and I always smile and answer that I got this intense power exactly on the day I read about desire and decided to believe in it and diverted my actions to achieve my definite goal.

The same day you choose to believe from your heart and soul that you have it, and the same day you believe you have it, you simply create the spirit to launch into action.

You cannot imagine how many times I use my will to direct this energy to overcome shame, laziness, fear, impatience, even anger or any other problem that is in my way to achieve my goals. I say all this not to show off my personal abilities, but to encourage you that this is possible for you if you decide to take control of your mind first.

I am currently finishing writing this book, but I am also preparing the next training event in Nairobi and working on the developing the courses as online courses. At the same time, I am lecturing for a couple of hours to university students and obviously developing new internet marketing skills, as I also enjoy working on social media and websites. I have a passion for all these tasks because I love to do them and every day I wake up with the spirit and the enthusiasm to work in each and all of them. I direct most of my power to my priorities which are myself, my family and my purpose to serve others through my company and its services. I know that the more power we direct into action, the more positive and forceful the action will be.

Before you engage in any action, get the spirit first. By expressing a kind desire for power for the matter you want to, you will get the spirit that keeps you enthusiastic and energetic during that matter or task ahead. You must enter into the spirit of whatever you are doing. When in recreation, for example, the mental attitude should still be there, authorising the body and mind to consciously relax; when at work, the spirit of adding value to your work and serving teammates, the organisation and its customer should be there supporting you with enthusiasm. This is very important for a leader, a manager or an employee, as the more spirited you become at work, the more spirited you become as a quality of your character.

The second important element when taking action is absolutely key: "feel successful" every time you take action. In fact, get this wrong and you'll be sure to at least delay the whole process.

Success-feeling must be cultivated using all techniques previously explained. My favourite one, imagination of course! Use it, imagine the desired outcome as if it was already achieved. Feel yourself filled with the confidence of greater and greater success. Be ready and get prepared to meet any obstacle; you are positive about life, but you know you will have to face some obstacles, so courage and determination must be cultivated on a daily basis and, more importantly, the purpose to always say...I will do it!.

Did you realise how many plans I already have in my mind? This is only for the next six months, why I do so? These are worthy plans that keep my mind busy and my actions focused. I am permanently implementing these plans through actions that I enjoy that keep me motivated and enthusiastic.

Now you will probably think that you normally take action and you do not need any of this energy or power and that is true; however, having this spirit makes things completely different as you are not reacting negatively to any obstacles but actually willingly go through them, you will never feel discouraged by any personal comment as you are always ready to move forward with very little distraction as your attention and concentration are fixed on your matter.

Moreover, as you develop this spirit, it naturally spreads into every action and aspect of your life. This transforms your life as you end up only seeing your final goal and virtually removing all the obstacles around it. At this moment, you become aware that simply working the way you have been doing surely will take you to your goal. It is only a matter of time. Doubts and fears completely disappear, the road is totally clean for you. This is the success feeling.

ACTING MINDFULLY

"Every act can be made strong and efficient by holding your vision while you are doing it, and putting the whole power of your Faith and Purpose into it."

-Wallace D. Wattles

1. Act now

Do what you have to do NOW, and be fully present when doing it. If you have a clear vision, the right mental attitude and the desire to do it, you have all you need to act. Delaying the process surely will have negative consequences for each of these elements; your desire could lose intensity, so you lose all the work you did to create that desire, and you will have to work harder to get to the same level of desire you had before; your mental attitude in turn will be weakened as your decreased desire could affect your "feeling-success" and the vision can become unclear.

This is what I experienced at the beginning of my journey and, curiously, it happened simply because I was achieving important goals and I started relaxing with some of my actions. One single call I should have done, and I procrastinated with, was enough to send a whole event into a 3 week "stand-by" status. This naturally had tremendous implications on the event's logistics and operations, which unfortunately ended up with a postponed event. It hit my mental attitude as I reacted negatively and try to fix it with a less positive attitude. I learned the first lesson of all lessons to be learned, not only in business but in life: ACT NOW. If an activity needs to be done today, ensure it is done today even if it can be postponed for another day. It seems like common sense, but you know...common sense is not so common most of the time.

2. Mental attitude and action should work together

I think this was, and still is, one of the hardest mental skills for me to master. I was unconsciously working harder as I was keeping a negative attitude while I was doing my work. All those negative feelings, worries, stress, fear and anxiety were present there when I was at work, which means I was never 100% involved in the activity I was working on. Of course, the result was never outstanding. There is a time when it is not only one or two activities that you don't particularly enjoy about your job, but it becomes the whole role. I know hundreds of people in this situation right now, usually complaining, "I do not like my job," "I want to work somewhere else," "I do not like being here" and I feel compassion for them and I am writing this book because of them.

Why this happens is because we have preferences. There are things that we like more that we prefer doing and there are others that we don't like so we want to avoid them. Ideally and according to one of my favourites book, "Teachings of a Buddhist Monk" by Ajahn Sumedho, the path of mindfulness is the path of no preferences. He said that "we should observe the kind of life that we have, whether we like it or not - it is changing anyway; it does not matter."

This isn't easy. We grow up with this mentality of having preferences and it seems to be part of our human nature. However, it doesn't mean that we cannot do anything about it. We can change how we react to the things and actions that we do not like doing.

We need to ensure that we perform each action with the right mental attitude. We cannot afford to have actions where we cannot control our feelings. To do this, first we ensure full awareness into all areas, including the activities we enjoy or do not like doing, so we can plan accordingly and ahead. We also need the awareness of our state of mind before doing the activity.

3. Putting the whole mind, soul and heart into the present action of your body

Be fully present, be fully aware, right there when you are taking actions. This is to be mindful, concentrating on what is happening inside you right when you are acting. Even more than that, you are proactively bringing your whole being into present action. I can tell you that it was really with this mindful action that I began to improve my productivity at work and I discovered a new sense of purpose in every little task I was doing. This made my work at that time more enjoyable and I noticed how each action was taking on a different meaning for me. I focused not only on the achievement of the task of my job, but also on the personal growth I could get out of each little task. It is incredible how a routine task was becoming more interesting for me when I took it as an opportunity for personal development by involving my mind, soul and heart into each action. I suddenly found myself training my mind and my will right there in my job. I stopped negative self-talk about my boring work and appreciates the opportunities I had for self-development more.

4. For every single action that you do, ensure you hold the vision of yourself and you do more than it is expected

Right now, while writing this book, I am practicing this point. I am usually monitoring that my mind is constantly contemplating my personal vision while I am writing. It gives me that sense of clear purpose. It keeps that feeling that I have a strong reason for doing it alive and, of course, it positively influences my level of desire not only to finish it but also to do my best. Sometimes I even have a picture or something that reminds me of my vision close to me and a quick look gives me that feeling that I am doing the right thing according to my ability, my purpose and my vision. I feel immediately motivated and this feeling guarantees that I continue working on it. I know many people who use this mental strategy as a powerful motivating force that works as a propulsion system to help them move forward, or even away from an undesired situation.

This is also a way to put spirit into the business life and enjoy work. If your employment is not directly related to your vision or purpose, if you feel that you need to move to other business in order to be fulfilled then you should ensure your vision is close to you while you make the transition to your preferred work.

I am fully convinced, due to my own experience, that if done appropriately, this step will encourage you to go the extra mile at work. I do not know if the desire for the achievement that produces this outcome or perhaps the willpower itself or simply your new mental attitude but when you keep your dream and purpose visually and mentally close to you, you will notice a tendency to give more than you used to give at work.

    5.   Each single action has to be effective and successful

"Let his work be well done." This is little sentence from the book "The Dhammapada" summarises this point. Observation, attention and concentration, all qualities of the mind that you can develop by training and practice, will support your work and ensure that you are not only fully present during the action but you have a higher expectation and higher standards to ensure an effective and successful action. Do not rush with actions; do not try to do more than one action at a time. Fewer actions done in a more efficient way is an old idea now, but still very relevant. Focus on the twenty percent that will make the most impact and ensure it is done efficiently. Do the work right and you will be recognised as a follower of righteousness.

A clear and focused vision together with a few minutes of total concentration on the task before starting will ensure a good beginning which can only be maintained by following all the previous four points. I would like to add to this point that the part of the "operational" goal of the self-development process that we discuss in this book is to make sure your actions are effective and successful because they are the result of a strong mindset that create the right mental attitude, a higher expectation and great habits. Really there should not be any other outcome.

    6.   Make each action a strong action by directing all your energy into it.

It is my greatest dream in concluding this book that you have felt the spirit in which I have written it and that you believe that you can develop the ability and grow yourself to become a person who lives a fulfilling life with a true purpose if you follow my suggestions.

I hope I have convinced you to believe in yourself and the possibilities that you have to grow to the highest potential you desire so you can follow you own self-development journey and make your own mark on the world.

7. Do each action with love, compassion and gratitude

This is the action I chose to end my book because it perhaps is the only message I have not talked about and I would like to refer it particularly to all managers and leaders in the world. As a leader or someone who is responsible for other people, in any circumstance, you do not have a job, you have a mission, you have a responsibility to your team or followers as important as the responsibility of a parent. Your team have been given to you and you have the beautiful opportunity to help them with their development as human beings. It is your opportunity to collaborate with the universe and with the co-creation of life. Be aware of the huge responsibility that you have to your people. To them first! Love, compassion and gratitude should be given to them first, independently of their performance and their results. Above all, we are human beings and our lives are far more important than the profit of any organisation. Unfortunately, our recent times and business culture have created a misconception, making us believe that profit maximisation is the ultimate goal and the purpose of every company or organisation. This idea couldn't be further from reality. We created companies for the benefits of all human beings; we created companies to improve the quality of our lives on this planet; that is the true. But this misunderstanding has changed the world, and it is not difficult to see that most employees, workers and managers are suffering. A great part of this suffering is due to their work and the imbalance with the other aspects of their lives. You, from your position or role, have the possibility, an amazing opportunity to change all this simply by giving human beings the place they really deserve in the organisation; the respectful treatment they deserve and the loving compassion that we all need. Commit to act with kindness to them, and ensure that in your mind there is truth and righteousness, non-violence, moderation and self-control in each of your actions and I can guarantee you will soon be the authentic and succesful leader of a great organisation.

THE END

ABOUT THE AUTHOR

Carlos Gomez was born in Barrancabermeja, Colombia, but has lived in London since 2003. He is married and has three daughters, aged 12, 9 and 8.

He attended Kingston University in the city, where he gained an MBA, and is currently the co-founder and director of BmitaGroup. He is also a speaker and trainer in International events in Africa, a personal coach, business consultant and a certified teacher of higher education in the UK.

Carlos has a deep interest in personal growth books and spends a lot of his free time reading as many of them as he can lay his hands on. He also loves to travel and has been to most of the continents and some unusual countries as a result of this.

His favorite quote is 'the very best thing you can do for the whole world is to make the most of yourself' and Carlos meditates on a daily basis in order to help achieve that end.

With his deep interest and incredibly detailed knowledge of the power of a clear mindset, Carlos decided to write his first book. The Clear Minded Leader is now available and is perfect for anyone who wants to become a better leader and who shares Carlos' vision.

In the future Carlos hopes that he and his book will inspire a new wave of authentic leaders from around the world and for them to create a change in the way we do things. He has already trained thousands of people in how to develop a strong mindset and he would like to continue this and become recognized as an international speaker. And of course, with this book he has become an international best-selling author too.

You can keep up with Carlos Gomez at the following;

cgomez@bmitagroup.com

Linkedin: https://uk.linkedin.com/in/carlosgomezafhea
Facebook: https://www.facebook.com/theClearmindedleader/
                https://www.facebook.com/carlos.j.gomez.754
Twitter: https://twitter.com/carlosgomezuk
Instagram: https://www.instagram.com/carlosgomeztcml/?hl=en
Amazon Author Page: https://www.amazon.co.uk/-
                /e/B01MTSL6N8

ONE LAST THING...

If you enjoyed this book or found it useful I'd be very grateful if you'd post a short review on Amazon. Your support really does make a difference and I read all the reviews personally so I can get your feedback and make this book even better.

If you'd like to leave a review then all you need to do is click the review link on this book's page on Amazon here:

https://www.amazon.co.uk/dp/B01N45CX0C/

Thanks again for your support!

Printed in Great Britain
by Amazon